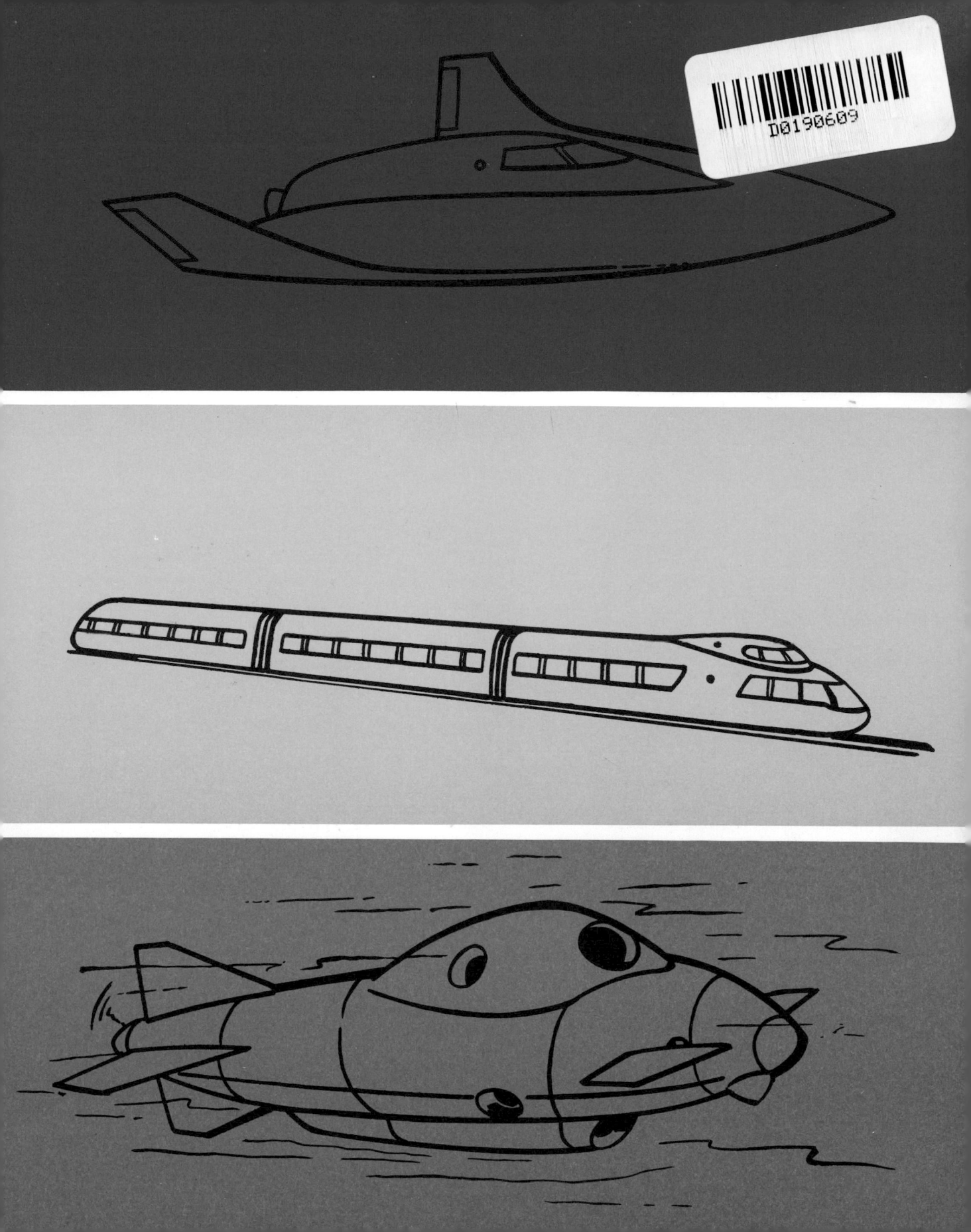

TRANSPORT
today and
tomorrow

J.M. Wilkinson.

Written by
John Day
Peter Duff
Michael Hill
Illustrated by
Gordon Davies

TRANSPORT
today and tomorrow

LUTTERWORTH PRESS   LONDON

First Published 1967

ACKNOWLEDGEMENTS

The publishers would like to thank the following for very kindly supplying photographs and information which were invaluable in the preparation of this book: British Railways; Great Northern Railways (U.S.A.); Italian, Japanese and French Railways; Alweg Monorail; Rover Car Co.; Ford Motor Co.; Scottish Aviation; Electricity Council.

Harland and Wolff Ltd.; Cunard Lines; P. and O. Orient Lines; Tyne-Tees Shipping Co. Ltd.; United States Lines; The Royal National Lifeboat Institute.

British European Airways; British Overseas Airways Corporation; Pan American Airways; Sikorsky Helicopters; British Aircraft Corporation; The Bristol Siddeley Journal.

Printed in Great Britain by
Fletcher & Son Ltd, Norwich

INTRODUCTION

Transport is something we all take for granted. There is always the family car, the bus at the end of the road, the railway station not far away, ships if we are going abroad on holiday, or aircraft flying swiftly from one airport to another. But it was not always like this. Just think of the changes someone like Sir Winston Churchill, living to the age of ninety, must have seen during his lifetime. Think of the changes you will see if you, in turn, live to that great age.

What, then, were things like in the 1870s when Winston Churchill was born. On the roads the horse was king everywhere, for long and short journeys, with a few people riding the new "bone-shaker" bicycle for short trips—the penny-farthing had not yet been invented. Roads were not always well kept in those days, for many people travelled by railways; giving speed and comfort unequalled by any other form of land transport, and by then already linking most important towns. The London Underground railway, the first in the world, had already been carrying passengers for a number of years and was expanding, but the world's first electric train did not come until the end of the seventies.

Mechanical transport by road had been tried, but the poor road surfaces and the weight of the steam engines which drove the vehicles defeated the attempts. Steam buses and coaches, however, had run from time to time since the 1830s, and steam tramway engines had already had some success, especially in Europe.

At sea the steamship had reached a stage similar to that of the railways, with all the main features of present-day design, including the screw propeller, already in use. Air transport did not really exist, though a balloon flight of over 1,000 miles had been made in the U.S.A. some years before, and several inventors were working on airships. Successful flight had to wait until the internal-combustion engine, designed in 1876 by Otto, had been brought to a high pitch of efficiency. The internal-combustion engine also made possible a whole string of new road vehicles, beginning with the crude cars and tricycles of the 1870s and 1880s and continuing down to the cars of the present day.

The railways today are faster, more comfortable than ever, but the car is so convenient that the train is more and more being used either for long overland journeys or to get to work in the great cities where the roads are too crowded to let buses and motor cars run as they should. The greatest change on the railways is the decline of steam power. You may travel from end to end of some countries and never see a steam locomotive. In others they are rare, in some they are still strong, but their time is running out and they are giving way swiftly to diesel or electric locomotives.

Freight trains are travelling at passenger train speeds and giving quicker service. Sometimes road vehicles, already

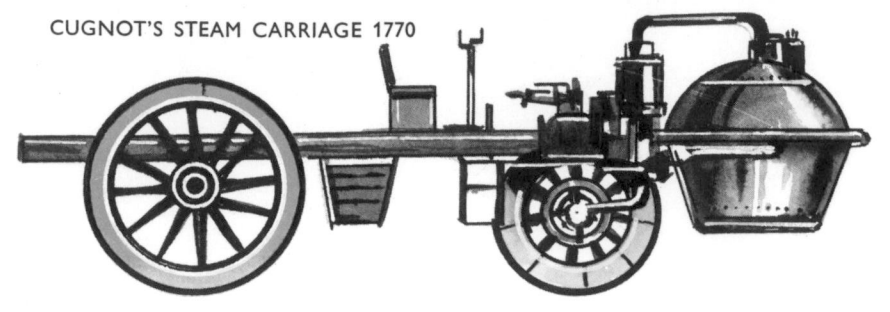

CUGNOT'S STEAM CARRIAGE 1770

STEPHENSON'S ROCKET 1829

THE FIRST *SAVANNAH* 1819

CUTTY SARK 1865

FIRST ELECTRIC LOCOMOTIVE 1879

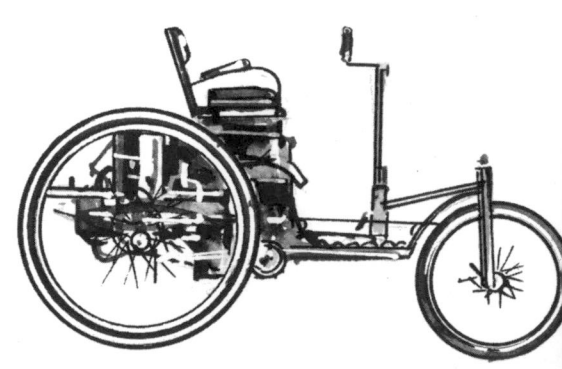

FIRST MOTOR-CAR CARL BENZ 1888

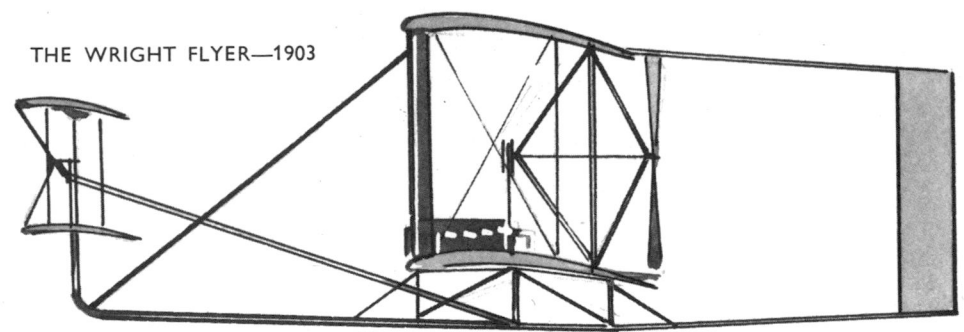

THE WRIGHT FLYER—1903

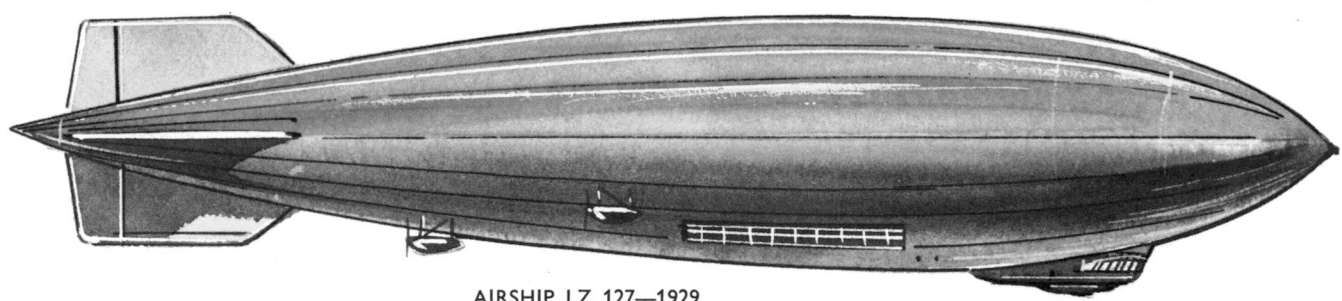

AIRSHIP LZ 127—1929

FAST BALTIC TYPE LOCOMOTIVE OF THE 1930s

D.H. COMET OF 1934

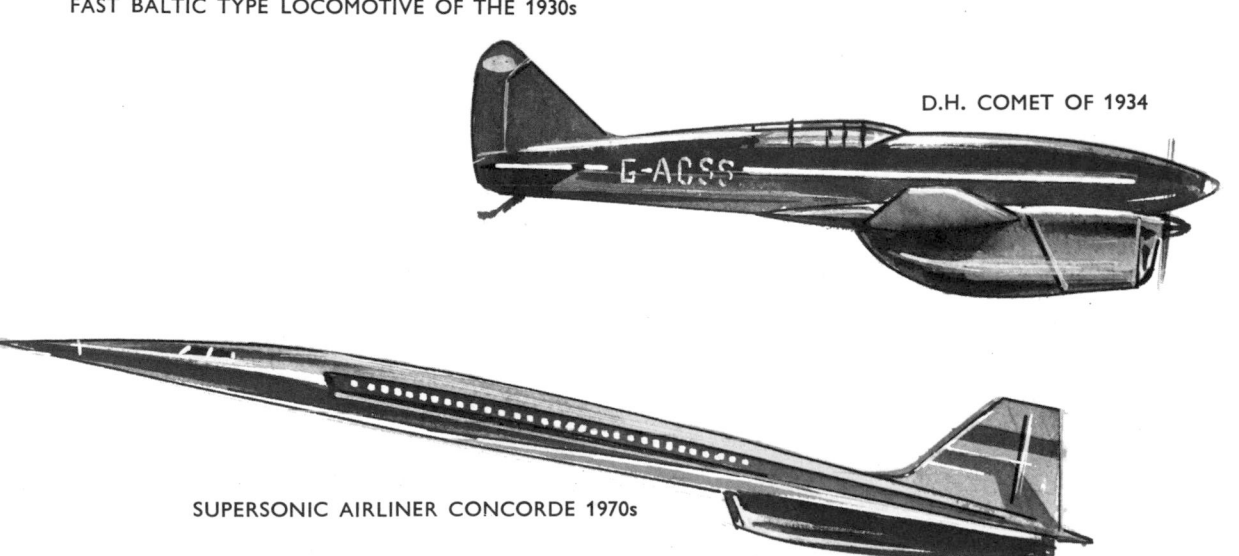

SUPERSONIC AIRLINER CONCORDE 1970s

loaded with freight, are driven on to trains, carried long distances on flat wagons, and driven off again to finish their journey by roads. Other trains carry freight in containers—large boxes like the bodies of trucks or railway wagons which can be carried on either vehicle. Wagons for carrying coal, ore, grain, and other things which do not need packing but can be carried in bulk are getting larger and larger.

At sea, the passenger vessel has come to a peak of luxury, speed and safety, but is giving way to giant aircraft which can make several journeys to its one. Cargo liners are getting bigger, faster, and more specialised.

Linking air and sea are the fast hovercraft riding on a cushion of air above the water. They are capable of travelling over land as well.

In the air itself, two world wars have hurried things along until even the ordinary passenger can expect speeds on long journeys of 500 or 600 m.p.h. Short flights may not be quite so fast, but are frequent. In the U.S.A. it is now possible to arrive at some airports, buy a ticket and board a waiting aircraft as though it was a bus or a train. Air freight is growing in importance for urgent goods and things which might spoil if the journey took too long. Car-carrying air ferries span the narrow seas between Great Britain and Europe.

We have just described what has happened over the last ninety years. What should we see if we went forward another ninety years to 2056? If progress goes on as fast as at present we could not even guess what we might see, but even so there are already signposts to the future.

On the railways many lines may be closed, but the great trunk lines linking the big cities will be improved.

On the roads, the long-distance car or coach will also be very fast and will have a network of highways or motorways on which to reach high speeds. On the highways they may be controlled and steered by impulses from cables buried under the centre of each lane, for the speeds will be too high to trust human drivers. As they leave the highway, control will be handed back to the driver but speed will be limited.

At sea the large freight vessel will probably still be running, possibly under automatic control with anti-collision radar but the passenger liner will probably—except for cruising—have given way to smaller, faster hydrofoil craft which will skim over the water at 100 m.p.h. with most of their hull far out of the water.

In the air, supersonic speeds will be the rule for intercontinental flights, and London—New York in two hours may be a standard schedule. For shorter flights, subsonic speeds will be cheaper, and probably 600 m.p.h. aircraft will be used with vertical take-off and descent so that airports can be smaller and nearer the centre of the cities they serve.

One thing is certain. Transport today, tomorrow and in the far future will always be the thread that ties man to man, country to country, and civilization to civilization. The purpose of transport will be the same even when it links, in the fullness of time, galaxy to galaxy.

John R. Day

LAND TRANSPORT

RAILWAYS

A railway, or railroad as it is called in the United States, is just a special sort of road. It began life, quite separately, in two places—the mines on the border between France and Germany and the coalfields of northern Britain. Wooden rails and small wooden trucks were used in Alsace 400 years and more ago, and about 300 years ago, when carts were used in the Tyneside coal-mining areas to carry coal from the pits to barges, someone had the idea of putting two rows of timber baulks down on the muddy cartways to make a hard surface on which the wheels could run. To keep the wheels on the timbers, the idea of making cartwheels shaped to fit the top of the baulks was tried, rendering them self-steering. The timber path made the carts so much easier to pull that the horses were able to do more work and pull heavier loads than ever before.

Later, the wooden timbers were faced with iron plates, making a plateway, hence the name "platelayer", still used in Britain for the man who looks after the railway tracks. Gradually the shapes evolved until at last there was an iron rail looking very much like those of today and the trucks had iron wheels with flanges to keep them on the rails. On such a railway—the Surrey Iron Railway—a horse pulled 55 tons for six miles in 1803. The same ease of movement of smooth wheels over smooth rails is still the reason for using railways today. Not only do railway vehicles move with little effort, but they also guide themselves. Nowadays steel rails are often welded into single lengths—sometimes several miles long. This cuts out the rail joints which give the typical rhythmic noise of the railway train, and allows a quiet, smooth

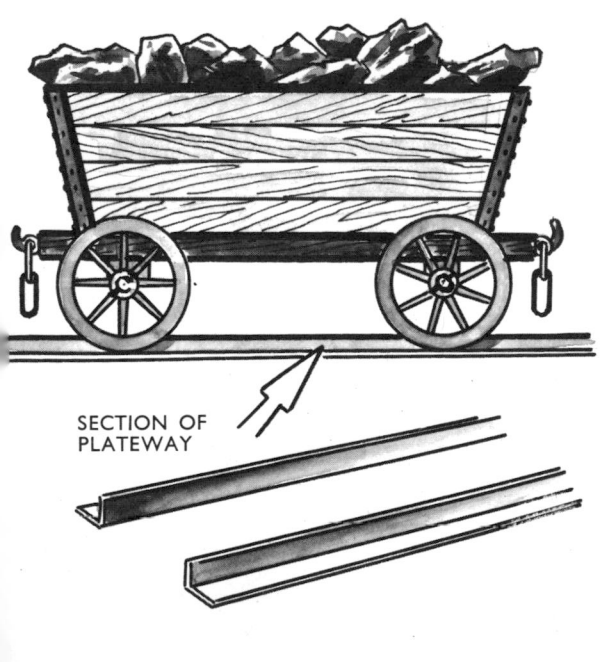

SECTION OF PLATEWAY

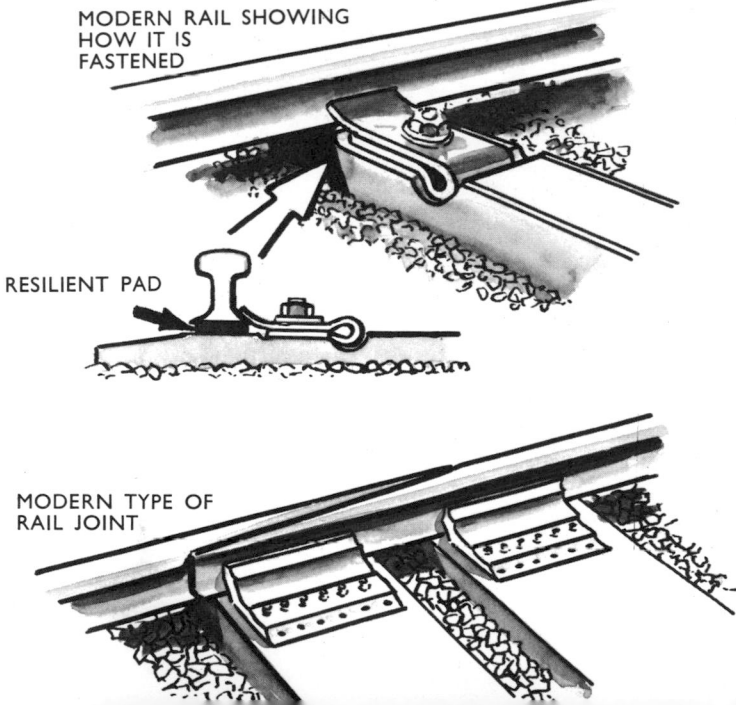

MODERN RAIL SHOWING HOW IT IS FASTENED

RESILIENT PAD

MODERN TYPE OF RAIL JOINT

Mountain railways are found in all parts of the world. In many cases a system of rack and pinions is needed to move coaches up steep mountain sides; ordinary wheels and rails would not provide sufficient grip. Here is one of the most famous of all mountain railways which runs up Mount Pilatus in Switzerland. It is the steepest rack and pinion railroad in the world; during a journey of between 2½ and 2¾ miles the track rises 5,344 feet. The picture clearly shows the vital rack and pinion system. The pinions (1 and 3) are fitted to the motors of the coach and grip on the rack (2) set between the running rails.

ride at any speed.

To hold the rails upright and the proper distance apart, sleepers or ties with fittings are laid beneath them. The first sleepers or ties were of timber, or possibly stone blocks, but nowadays wood, steel or concrete are the usual materials, with concrete coming more and more into favour.

Ideas about the distance the rails should be apart—the track gauge—vary. Early British lines took their gauge from the coal carts, sometimes still called the "coal-cart gauge". Set by chance at the odd figure of 4 ft. $8\frac{1}{2}$ in., it has been copied by many countries, and is usually called the standard gauge. It is used in most parts of the U.S.A., Europe, Great Britain, Canada, North Africa, China and other countries. A wider gauge is adopted in other places, such as in Russia with 5 ft., in Ireland with 5 ft. 3 in., and in India and Pakistan with much 5 ft. 6 in. track. In hilly country it is cheaper to build a narrower gauge, so that South Africa, New Zealand, much of Japan and other countries use the 3 ft. 6 in. gauge. Very narrow gauges, down to 2 ft., were used for railways where lines had to be laid cheaply or on difficult routes.

The custom of trains keeping to the left is also copied from Britain even in countries where road traffic keeps to the right. Exceptions include Russia and North America, where rail traffic keeps to the right.

A locomotive needs to be heavy to make the wheels grip on the rails or give adhesion. If the railway has to climb a hill, the line must be built with a very

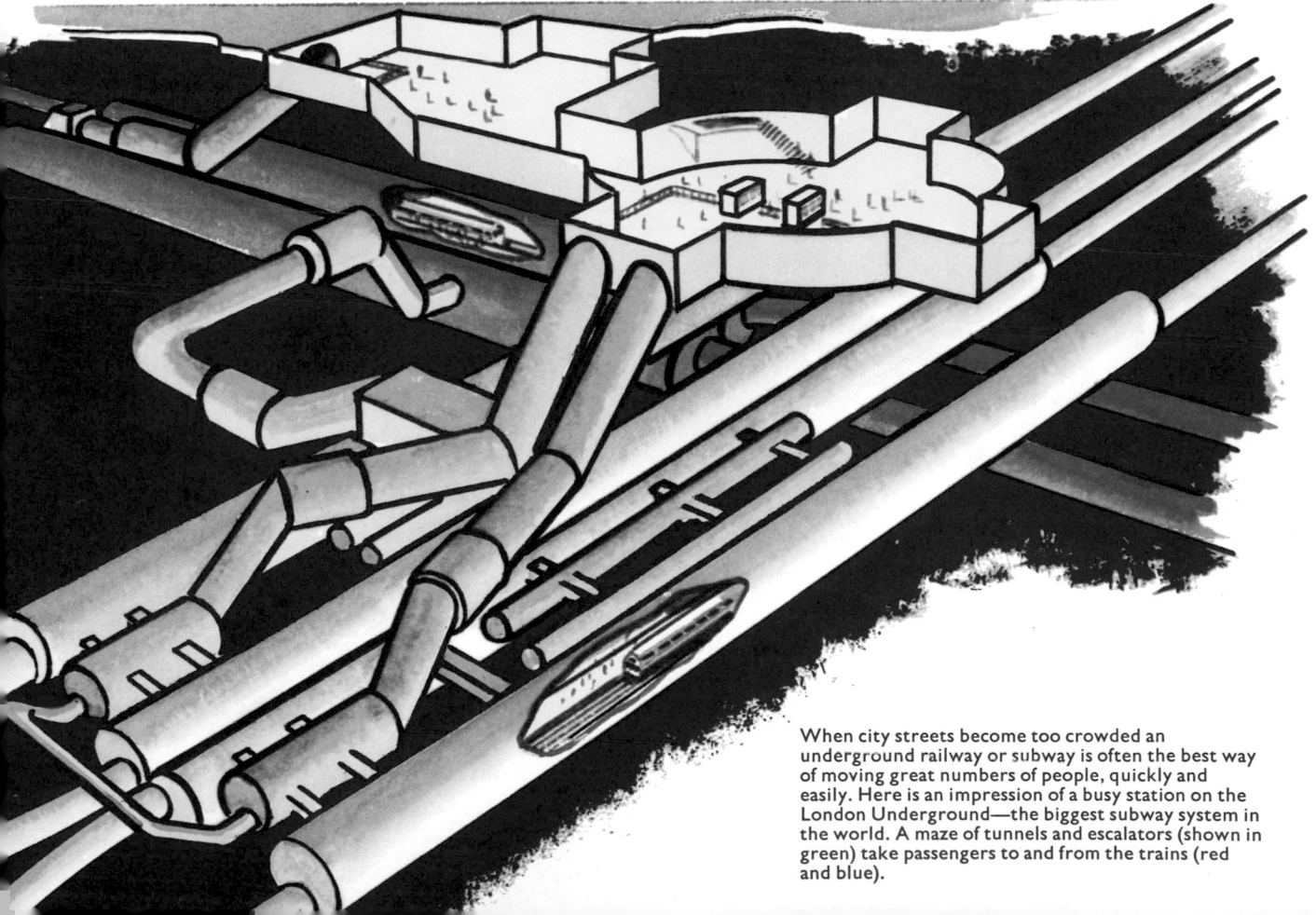

When city streets become too crowded an underground railway or subway is often the best way of moving great numbers of people, quickly and easily. Here is an impression of a busy station on the London Underground—the biggest subway system in the world. A maze of tunnels and escalators (shown in green) take passengers to and from the trains (red and blue).

gentle slope or the locomotive wheels will spin round without gripping the track. This is why there are so many tunnels, cuttings and embankments on rail routes —to keep the track as level as possible so that heavy trains can be hauled. Careful planning can enable great heights to be reached. The Peruvian Central Railroad has a standard gauge line which reaches 15,848 ft.

In countries with high mountains and deep valleys, such as Switzerland, railways must be able to climb steep slopes. This is made possible by fitting a metal bar with teeth cut into it, called the rack rail, between the rails. The locomotive is fitted with one or more special toothed driving wheels, called pinions, the teeth being cut to fit into the rack. On steep sections the toothed wheel engages the rack to give a firm grip. On mountain railways the whole line may have the rack rail, of which there are several types. One of the steepest rack railways is the Pilatus Railway near Lucerne, which in places climbs 1 ft. for every 2 ft. of track. Even steeper railways are built and used for passenger and sometimes freight traffic, but with these the railway cars are hauled by cables. The steepest of these funicular railways, as they are called, rises 1 ft. for every 1 ft. $1\frac{1}{2}$ in. of track.

Railways can carry many people quickly and safely, and trains can follow close behind each other. With good signalling, trains can be run every 90 seconds, and one railway track can carry 40,000 or so people an hour. No other form of transport can do this and it is natural that railways should be used to carry the people who flock into the great cities of the world every morning to work and leave them again in the evening.

Underground Railways

There is little room in cities for ordinary railroads, and the answer, thought of nearly 140 years ago in the very early days of railways, is to put the line underground. The world's first underground railway, the Metropolitan, opened in London in 1863. It had steam trains and, although smoke made conditions unpleasant sometimes, was a great success. To avoid damage to buildings, nearly all this railway was built under roads by digging a deep trench, putting the rails in a brick tunnel, and replacing the road back on top. This is called "cut-and-cover" construction and is still used in many countries.

Electric trains allowed some later railways, especially in London, to be built deep down by using a tubular shield in which men can work to cut a tunnel for the subway. Such shields sometimes have mechanical cutting equipment. The tunnel, in the shape of a tube, is lined with rings of iron or concrete to prevent the earth falling in after the shield has passed. In London, more than a yard of tunnel an hour has been built in this way by one mechanical shield and its small crew.

There are also subways in New York, Chicago, Toronto, Paris, Berlin, Hamburg, Rome, Milan, Madrid, Barcelona, Lisbon, Stockholm, Moscow, Leningrad, Tokyo, Osaka, Buenos Aires and some other large cities. More are being planned every year, especially in the U.S.A. where a super-subway is being built in the San Francisco Bay area.

Underground lines often rise to the

Two six-car units of the Alweg monorail, which runs from Tokyo to Haneda in Japan, meet over Tokyo Bay.

surface on the outskirts of cities where land is less valuable.

All railway trains have one important thing in common. No matter how long they are, and how much they carry, only two men need be in charge—one on the locomotive and a guard or conductor —sometimes even one will do.

Monorails

In towns, there has been a revival of interest in the monorail. Monorail means "one rail", and the original system patented in 1821 by Henry Robinson Palmer, an Englishman, did have only one raised rail. The cars were divided so that half hung down on each side of the rail, giving a natural balance. Some inventors later used gyroscopes to keep cars balanced upright on top of a single rail, but balance was always a problem, and later monorail

systems had three or even five rails. The extra rails were used to guide or balance the cars.

At Eberfeld, in Germany, a successful monorail for passenger traffic was opened in 1901. It was to a system invented by Eugen Langen, a Cologne engineer, in which the cars hung below a single-rail track. There were tracks for each direction and the monorail was later extended until it was over eight miles long. It is still working safely today.

Two modern systems are the French Safege, which has cars hung from a rubber-tyred bogie running on twin tracks inside a box girder open at the bottom, and the German Alweg, which has cars straddling a concrete beam. Rubber-tyred wheels run on top of the beam to carry and drive the cars, and two sets of wheels run on each side of the beam

The monorail may help to solve the traffic problem in modern cities. Riding on a single concrete beam the Alweg monorail system carries passengers in Seattle, Disneyland, Tokyo, and Turin (shown above).

to balance and steer it. There are short Alweg lines in Seattle and Disneyland, in Turin, Italy, in Japan—including an eight-mile line between Tokyo and its airport—and elsewhere. Many people advocate monorail lines such as these for city transport.

The diagram (left) shows a section of a monorail coach. The driving and suspension wheels run on top of the concrete "rail". The side wheels help to balance the coach and keep it steady.

A modern diesel-electric locomotive for Finnish Railways. Designed and built in France by the Société Alsthom, it develops 2,800 h.p. and is used for both passenger and freight services. The two diesel motors (**1** and **2**) drive electric generators (**3** and **4**) which provide current for the drive motors in the bogies (**5** and **6**). The electrical control panel (**7**) is mounted in the centre of the locomotive between the generators, and the radiators for the drive motors can be seen on the side panel (**8**).

ENGLISH ELECTRIC DELTIC

CANADIAN NATIONAL DIESEL

AUSTRALIAN—QUEENSLAND
GOVERNMENT LOCOMOTIVE

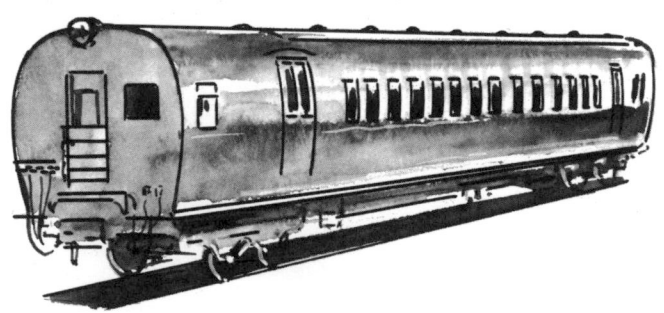

BRAZILIAN MOTOR COACH

Railway Motive Power

On early railways, wagons were pushed by hand, but, later, horses took over. Steam power came along at the very beginning of the nineteenth century—the first steam locomotive, built by Richard Trevithick, pulled its first train in 1804—but was not used for hauling all types of trains until the opening of the Liverpool and Manchester Railway in 1830 at the beginning of the railway age. From George and Robert Stephenson's *Rocket* of 1829 onwards, steam made rapid progress, reaching a peak of power and speed in the 1930s. It was on July 3, 1938 that the British Pacific type locomotive *Mallard* set up a world record speed for steam locomotives of 126 m.p.h. on a section of the East Coast main line between London and Scotland. In the U.S.A., the Union Pacific's "Big Boy" locomotives weighed with tenders, 540 tons.

By this time the two main challengers to steam were well-developed. The first oil-engined locomotive, a small four-wheel machine designed by William Priestman, ran in Hull, England, in 1892. Then came some 20 h.p. locomotives to designs patented by Akroyd Stuart in 1890, also in Britain. Just before the First World War there appeared an experimental locomotive of 1,000 h.p. to the designs of Dr. Rudolf Diesel, and subsequently the name Diesel was applied to all locomotives of this type. He built this first locomotive in 1912, but registered his patents earlier, in 1894.

Diesel development began again after the First World War. One of the first great successes was the *Flying Hamburger* twin railcar in Germany, which ran regular services in 1933 between Berlin and Hamburg at an average speed of 77·4 m.p.h. Not many trains do this even today. In 1939 a German diesel train reached $133\frac{1}{2}$ m.p.h.

Most of the pioneer work on diesels was done in Europe, but the wide acceptance of these new locomotives was largely due to the U.S.A., which, having good supplies of oil, built very large numbers of the various sizes needed for railway purposes. In Europe, after the Second World War, when many new locomotives were needed, diesel locomotives were generally preferred to steam and few new steam units are being built today.

Diesel locomotives have several advantages over steam, apart from being cleaner in every way. They can be coupled together to work heavier trains, and the two or more locomotives can all be controlled by a single crew. Steam locomotives have to go to the depot for attention every day, but diesels need less maintenance—some shunting engines go to the depot only once a week. Diesels can produce high power for their weight and can make up time quickly if stopped at signals and run at steady speeds over long distances. Full power is available at the movement of a lever. Being self-contained units, diesels can be used, just as they are, to replace steam locomotives.

The use of electric power, the other main challenger to steam, is not a matter of replacing one type of machine by another. The electric locomotive is not self-contained: It picks up power produced in a generating station and carried to the point where it is collected by the train. Current distribution to trains needs either many short sections of track, each

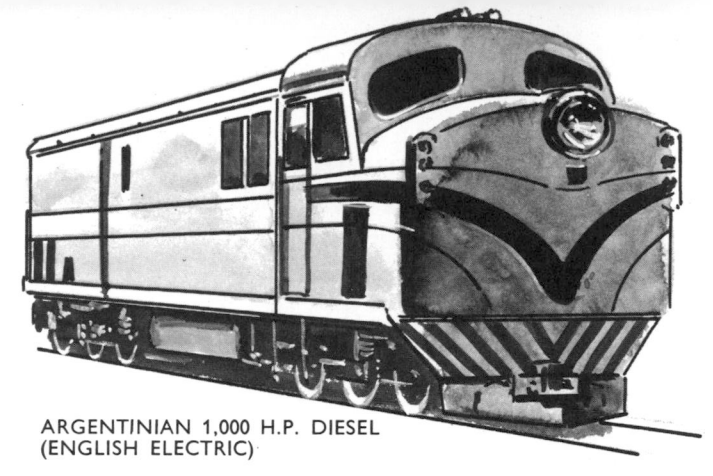

ARGENTINIAN 1,000 H.P. DIESEL
(ENGLISH ELECTRIC)

BRITISH RAILWAYS MIXED
TRAFFIC 1,000 H.P. DIESEL

BRITISH 380 H.P. DIESEL FOR NATIONAL COAL BOARD

FRENCH ALSTHOM C.C. 40 ELECTRIC

a few miles long, fed by a substation which takes electricity from the generating station at high voltage and passes it out to the trains at low voltage, or longer sections fed at very high voltage. The first method is used with direct current —current which flows constantly in one direction—at voltages of up to about 1,500. The current can be passed through conductor rails, from which it is picked up by collector shoes on the train, at up to about 750 V. Above that voltage it is usual to use overhead wires from which the power is taken by a collector on the locomotive or train roof. The return circuit to the substation is through the running rails.

High-voltage alternating current is sent along overhead wires for much greater distances. This type of current flows in a series of waves, starting with no current in the wire, building up to a peak in one direction, dying away to nothing, and then rising to a peak in the opposite direction. This is a very rapid process and in most countries, where electricity of this type is supplied to factories and houses, the fluctuation or cycle takes place 50 times a second.

Because the cost of electrification of a railway is high, as many trains as possible use the electrified section once it is completed, and other, less efficient, routes are closed down. So that the one line can take many extra trains; improvements of other kinds have to be made, especially to the track and the signalling system. All this adds to the cost of electrification. A busy electrified line, however, is the most efficient form of railway.

Not all trains have locomotives. Many passenger trains have several diesel or electric motors mounted on coaches down the length of the train and all controlled from a driver's cab in the front coach; these are called multiple-unit trains. Suburban and underground trains are often of this type, but it is also gaining in popularity for long-distance trains like the very fast Trans-Europe Expresses linking European capitals and other major cities. They can be driven by one man.

Many diesel multiple-unit trains and locomotives are driven by electric motors in the same way as electric trains, the diesel motor driving a generator to provide the electricity as though each train had its own generating station. Other diesels have hydraulic transmission, the motor driving a type of turbine-in-reverse to give energy to a fluid which drives another turbine and, in turn, the wheels. Low-powered diesels sometimes have mechanical transmission through gears very like those of a bus or lorry. The more complicated drives are needed to enable the best use to be made of the motor which, like that of the automobile produces its greatest power when it is running at high speed.

The "Empire Builder" is one of the most famous trains in the United States. It speeds along the Great Northern Railway route from Chicago to Seattle and Portland. Included in the train layout are Great Dome coaches like the one in the picture. They are double-deck coaches 85 feet in length over buffers and are carried on two six-wheeled trucks. The top deck observation lounge (1) with its clear dome (2) has seats for 74 passengers. The lounge section with its bar on the lower deck (3) holds 34 passengers. An air conditioning unit (4) controls the ventilation.

Gas-turbine locomotives, in which hot gases from burning fuel drive a turbine, have been tried in Europe, the U.S.S.R. and the U.S.A. They have not made much headway against the diesel unit, but there are, for example, some very powerful, quite successful locomotives hauling long-distance heavy freight trains on the Union Pacific Railroad. Gas-turbine locomotives elsewhere are generally of an experimental nature.

Two other inventions of which much may be heard in the future are the fuel cell and the linear motor. The fuel cell is a device now under development which allows the energy of fuel to be converted directly to electrical energy, cutting out the intermediate stages of engine and generator. This process wastes much less of the fuel's energy than conventional methods and may one day give a light, fairly simple, and cheap alternative to the diesel engine. The linear motor is an electric motor which has no moving parts. The greater part of the motor, including the windings and poles, is mounted on the train, and the rest, consisting of a continuous metal plate, is laid between the railway lines. Present indications are that this motor would be best suited to high-speed trains. There are plans for "hovertrains" which would be supported a fraction of an inch above the rails by a cushion of air and driven by linear motors at speeds of two or three hundred miles an hour.

On one-man driven diesel and electric trains, in particular, devices are fitted to stop the train should the driver become ill. One of the best-known devices is the "dead-man's handle", which the driver has to keep pressed down, but there are other systems. Many locomotives have vigilance devices which stop the train unless the driver takes some form of action after the sounding of a warning.

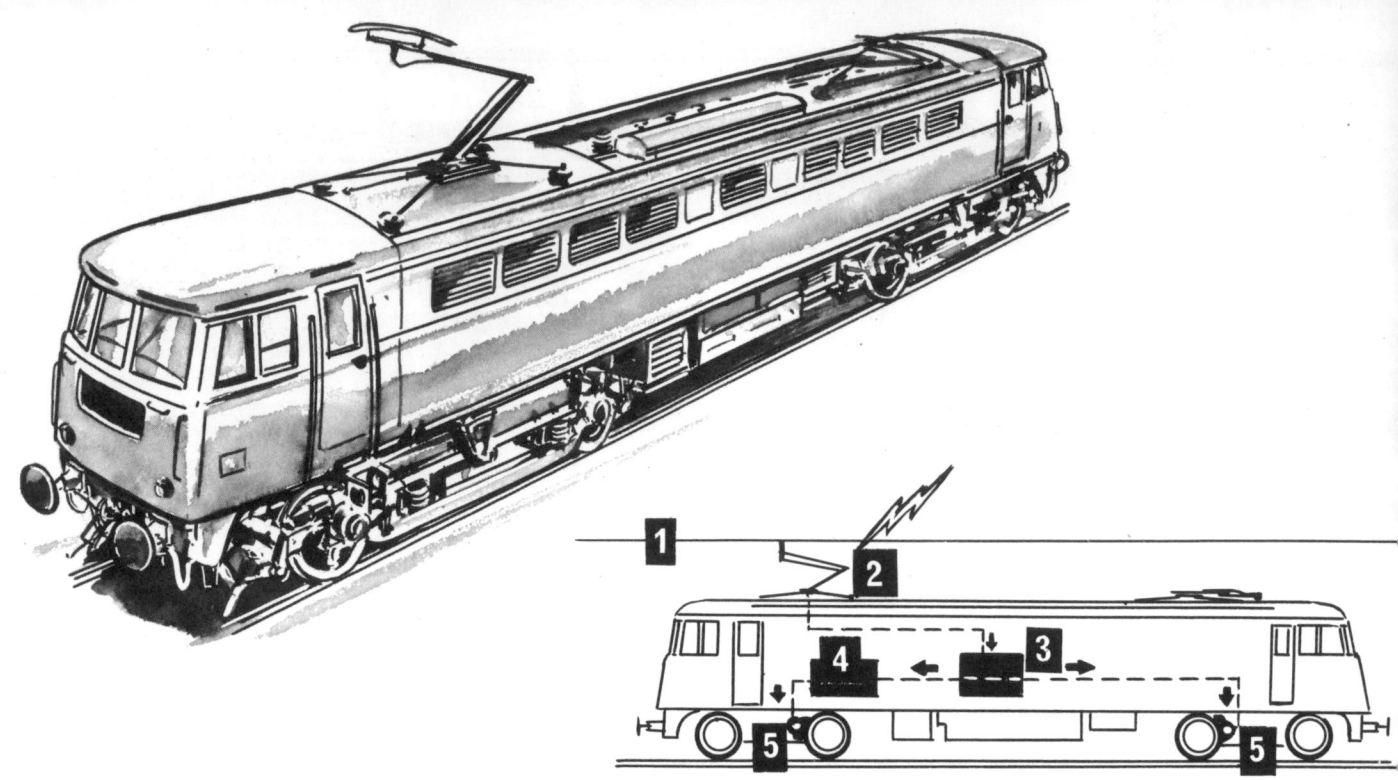

An electric locomotive; the diagram shows: **1.** The conductor cable. **2.** The pick-up. **3.** Transformer. **4.** Rectifier. **5.** The power bogies.

Passenger Trains

It was not until the 1830s that any special thought was given to passenger travel by rail. The Liverpool and Manchester Railway had covered first-class coaches in 1830, and open coaches for other passengers, but it was not until many years later that all passengers had a roof over their heads. The early coaches were small and had only four wheels, but as passenger traffic grew, bigger vehicles were needed, and the number of wheels was increased to six and then to eight. An eight-wheeled coach, even with the wheels grouped in fours at each end, was too rigid to go round tight curves, so the bogie came into being. This is a short four- or six-wheeled truck with a pin in the centre on which one end of the coach

is mounted. The short trucks can go round curves easily with the coach body supported by, and swivelling on, two of them.

Corridors in the centre or at the side of coaches, with connections over the gap between them, made it possible for passengers to move about the train. Pullman cars with sleeping berths were introduced by George Mortimer Pullman in the United States in 1859. Meals could be had at main stations, where trains made a long halt for the purpose, and eventually dining cars were attached to the trains themselves. Today, long-distance trains may have not only dining and sleeping cars, but also lounges, buffets and bars, telephone booths with radio connection to the national telephone system, upperdeck or tail-end observation lounges with panoramic views of the surrounding

20

countryside, bathrooms, hairdressing saloons, shops and even cinemas. All have very comfortable seats with good lighting and heating, and some have proper air-conditioning which cools the air in summer as well as warming it in winter.

All this luxury is provided because train travel must be attractive to compete with other forms of transport. The train must be able to show a great advantage in speed and comfort to persuade owners to leave their cars behind. Over longer distances the train must compete with the aeroplane. Most airports are outside the cities they serve, so to the length of the air journey must be added the time taken to get to and from the airports. Railways usually have the advantage of stations near city centres and this means that for distances of, say, 200 miles, and sometimes a good deal more, the total time taken by the train is no more than that of the air journey. Over really long distances, the train's only attraction, like that of the ocean liner, is its extra comfort compared with air travel.

Trains which carry people to work in cities, the suburban trains, do not need the same comfort, for journeys in them rarely last more than an hour. They do need as many seats as possible and plenty of doors to let people in and out quickly. Underground or subway trains which take people into the city centre itself carry very many passengers on journeys lasting only 15–20 minutes or less. They are therefore designed with a few seats for long-distance passengers and plenty of standing space for rush-hour passengers. The doors are wide and often worked by power under the control of the guard or driver.

Main line trains, which may make journeys lasting from one hour to several days, range from fast electrical and diesel sets to trains like the *Empire Builder* of the Great Northern Railway in the United States. This is not a fast train—it takes nearly 44 hours to run from Chicago in the Middle West to Seattle on the Pacific Coast, 2,210 miles away, but it is one of the world's most comfortable and luxurious trains. To ride in it is such an experience that many people prefer it to the faster aeroplane. In Europe, the Trans-Europe expresses run at consistently high speeds, but there are also trains like the *Settebello* in Italy, which covers the 394 miles from Rome to Milan in 6 hours. In Britain, the 393-mile London–Edinburgh run is covered in 6 hours. The world's railways are realising the importance of fast trains, and 100 m.p.h. trains may soon be commonplace. In Japan, streamlined expresses are running regularly on the new Tokaido line at 125 m.p.h., and could run even faster.

Trains may sometimes be carried across stretches of water by ferry without disturbing the passengers. For example, the "Night Ferry" from London enables the traveller to get into bed in London and wake up in France, the train having been gently shunted on to a ferry ship for the Channel crossing.

The railways compete with motor cars but also give special services for motorists. Some carry driver, passengers and motor cars over long distances to save time on holiday trips. In the Alps, another service to motorists is given through some of the long railway tunnels. The motorist drives on to a train of flat wagons near one entrance to the tunnel, is carried through on the train, and drives off at the other end of the tunnel. This saves all the strain imposed on car and driver by driving over the Alpine passes. Passengers on these services usually remain in the car.

Attempts have been made in the past to fit railway vehicles with pneumatic tyres with the idea of increasing comfort and reducing noise. Because the weight is concentrated on the narrow rails, many wheels must be used and even then the tyres wear quickly, so such attempts have so far failed. The Paris underground, the Metro, uses rubber-tyred trains on some of its lines, using special tracks and keeping the steel rails only to guide the vehicles. Among the advantages claimed are quicker acceleration and braking because the rubber tyres grip the track firmly, and silent running. The Montreal and Haifa Subways, planned with French technical help, also have pneumatic-tyred trains. The Haifa Subway is a funicular railway in a tunnel.

Methods of Moving Freight

At one time the open wagon was the only railway vehicle, but nowadays railways use wagons designed for carrying particular types of freight whenever there is enough of that type to make it worth while. They also have special equipment for loading and unloading. For traffic in small units, the tendency is to use methods which enable goods to be packed before their journey begins and to remain untouched until they arrive at their destination.

An example of bulk traffic is coal, which for many years has been carried in

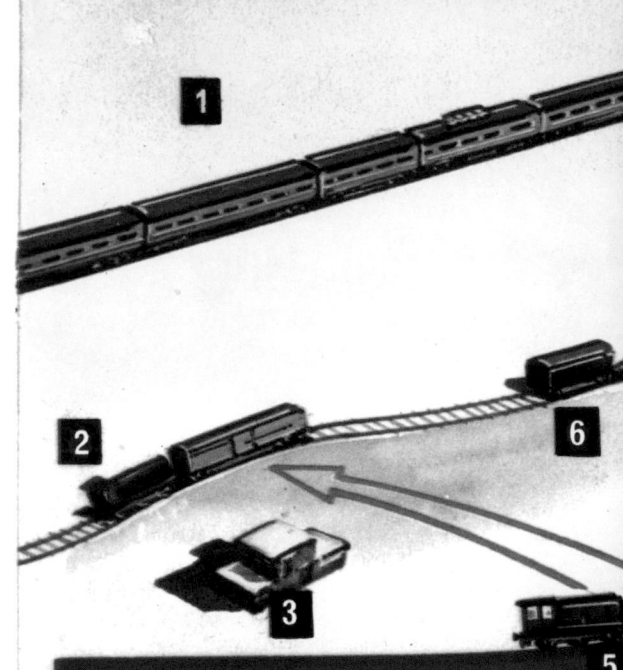

special trains. Small wagons from which the coal had to be hand-shovelled have given way to big ones with hoppers and doors which allow the coal to be discharged in one minute. The latest development in Britain is the "merry-go-round" train, consisting of large specially-designed wagons coupled permanently together and running regularly between two points specially equipped for this kind of train. The doors of the wagons are opened automatically as they come to the unloading point and closed as they pass on. Coal is loaded into them from above. These trains never stop, but move at a very low, steady speed while loading and unloading, processes taking 90 and 60 minutes for trains made up of 32-ton capacity, bottom-discharged, hopper wagons and carrying 1,000 tons of coal in all. These trains are capable of three 70-mile round trips a day. Bulk trains of this or a similar nature are coming to the fore in most countries.

Coal and ore wagons can also be un-

A marshalling yard. The numbers inset show: **1.** Main line. **2.** Diesel-electric shunting locomotive. **3.** Shunting control cabin. **4.** Truck running down hump on its way to the appropriate siding. **5.** Shows how the shunting loco. pushes the trucks to the top of the hump. **6.** A truck on its way down. **7.** Hump. **8.** Many tracks fanning out, each controlled by points operated from the shunting control cabin. **9.** Retarders.

loaded by tipplers, which clamp the wagon firmly and raise one end or side so that the load falls out of the end or side doors. Some tipplers pick the wagon up bodily and turn it upside down.

Special wagons need not necessarily run in trains made up of one type of wagon. Steel-carrying wagons, for example, can travel in special trains from a steelworks to a sorting yard and then be sent off individually, in ordinary freight trains, to their final destination. Oil tank, bulk cement, fish, banana, grain, cattle, refrigerator and motor car wagons are other examples. Other individual modern wagon types include vehicles with sprung bodies able to absorb shocks, open wagons with metal roller shutters to cover them when required, and wagons with opening roof doors. In the latest cement wagons, the powder is loaded in bulk through pipes or chutes into the airtight body of the wagon. At the destination compressed air is used to force the cement powder out again through pipes—sometimes into a similarly equipped road vehicle which makes the final delivery to the site.

Refrigerator wagons may use solid carbon dioxide or "dry ice", real ice, or built-in diesel-driven refrigerating machinery to keep their loads cold. Tank wagons are sometimes giants carrying 100 tons or more, especially in the United States. A train of these carries as much as an oil tanker would sailing into

23

the heart of the countryside—and is much faster. Other tank wagons, may range from similar giants to small tanks which can be lifted or slid from road to rail vehicles—or even be made of flexible materials so that they can be rolled up when empty—can carry liquids such as milk, edible oils, chemicals, molasses, and even liquid gases, such as butane or propane, under pressure.

For smaller goods, the great development has been in container traffic and the basically similar "piggy-back" services. A container is a special form of packing case which may be of steel, wood or plastics and range in size from a small box to that of a lorry or railway wagon body. Containers may be plain, insulated, refrigerated, heated, fitted with a variety of racks, open, closed, rigid or folding so as to take up less space when returned empty.

A factory sending a load of small items can have a railway container brought to the door by truck. The goods are then packed at the factory and the container is sealed and taken by road to the nearest suitable railway depot where it is transferred to a railway wagon to make a high-speed run over the main part of its journey, perhaps by an express "liner" train running to a fixed timetable every night. At the destination depot the container is again transferred and it is taken to its destination by road. There the goods, still in their factory wrappings, are unpacked.

Piggy-back traffic is similar, except that in this case the container consists of a complete road trailer, wheels included. This system is especially popular in America, where high bridges and tunnels give more clearance than in Europe for high loads. In the United States, the trailers are carried on flat wagons, but in Europe special wagons are needed to reduce the load height by using a form of pocket to take the wheels. In some versions, the wheels are removed from the trailer before it is loaded and a spare set is fitted at the other end. The piggy-back system, now so popular, is a century old and seems to have been begun by the English general manager of the Buenos Aires Great Southern Railway, as it then was. He used low wagons to carry bullock carts full of wool on their journeys to market, cutting out handling and reloading.

In the United States and Great Britain, there are some road trailers with two sets of wheels. They are hauled over the roads to a railway depot and placed astride the rails. Then a small motor lowers a set of railway wheels on to the track and raises the road wheels clear. Joined together in trains, these special vans can make high-speed runs over railway tracks behind a locomotive and can be converted quickly for road use again at the other end of the rail run.

Railways also have a few special wagons for carrying very heavy items such as electrical transformers, boilers, and towers for refining plants which cannot be broken down into smaller sections. Such wagons may have 20 axles and be capable of carrying upwards of 300 tons. Sometimes the whole wagon body, complete with load, can be transferred to road bogies so that the load can remain undisturbed from door to door on its slow journey.

Freight wagons. Left is a 16 ton Speedfreight wagon of British Railways (L.M.R.).

Two American freight wagons. Above a 23,450-gallon tank car and right a giant covered hopper car designed to carry up to 190,000 pounds of grain.

Marshalling Yards

Although through trains are run where there is enough traffic to fill them, many wagons still have to make part of their journey on one train and then be transferred to another going in the right direction. Sometimes several changes of train are needed. Modern methods of sorting wagons cut down the time taken by this process to a fraction of what it used to be. In a hump marshalling yard a train of wagons, uncoupled, is pushed up a slope to the top of a hump. On the other side the track falls away steeply so that wagons gather speed quickly and are separated by some distance from the wagon behind. As the wagon rolls down the slope, sets of points are turned from a control tower—often automatically according to a programme prepared in advance—so that the wagon is directed on to one of many tracks, each of which contains wagons for a particular area.

To make sure that the wagon reaches the right track but does not collide heavily with wagons already on it, the speed must be controlled. This is done by retarders which apply braking pressure to the sides of the wheels as the wagons run through them. The degree of pressure depends on the speed of the wagon and how far it has to run. In modern yards the speed and weight of the wagon are measured automatically as it approaches the retarder. These figures are fed into a computer, together with information on the number of wagons already on the track concerned, the braking effect of the track on the way to it, and the prevailing wind pressure. The computer then calculates, in the time taken for the wagon

to roll a yard or two, exactly how much pressure to apply.

Railway Signalling and Control

A fast train cannot pass a slow one on the same track, so trains must follow one another until they can be switched on to different tracks. Also, the great weight of a train—some mineral trains go up to 5,000 tons or more, and trains up to 14,000 tons are planned—and the lack of friction between steel wheels and rails makes it impossible for it to stop quickly. An express train may need a mile in which to stop. This means that some form of advance warning is needed to prevent collisions, and trains must be moved from one track to another as required.

The need for a warning system became clear in the early days of railways, even though there were only a few trains, well spaced out, during the day. At junctions trains would stop to make sure that no other train was in sight before going on. Sometimes they were ordered by the timetable to wait until a certain train had passed, even though that train might be hours late.

Some odd ways of showing whether the line ahead was clear were used in those days. On the Stockton and Hartlepool line a candle was put in a station window if it was necessary for a train to stop. Other railways used baskets on poles, still others large coloured flags.

Then came the railway policemen in their top hats and tail coats. They stood at junctions and "police stations" with outstretched arms to show drivers that the line was clear. When it was not clear, they stood at ease. At night they used coloured lamps, and later they began to use coloured flags or painted boards by day. These boards or flags could be positioned to show the state of the track ahead and left in place while the policeman attended to the board for another line. In time, ropes and wires were used to change the boards from a distance and

these show the state of the next stop signal and warn drivers that they must be prepared to stop at the next signal ahead. The origin of this type of signal, which uses coloured lamps at night—red for danger, yellow for caution and green for clear—explains why many older railway

TYPES OF SIGNALS

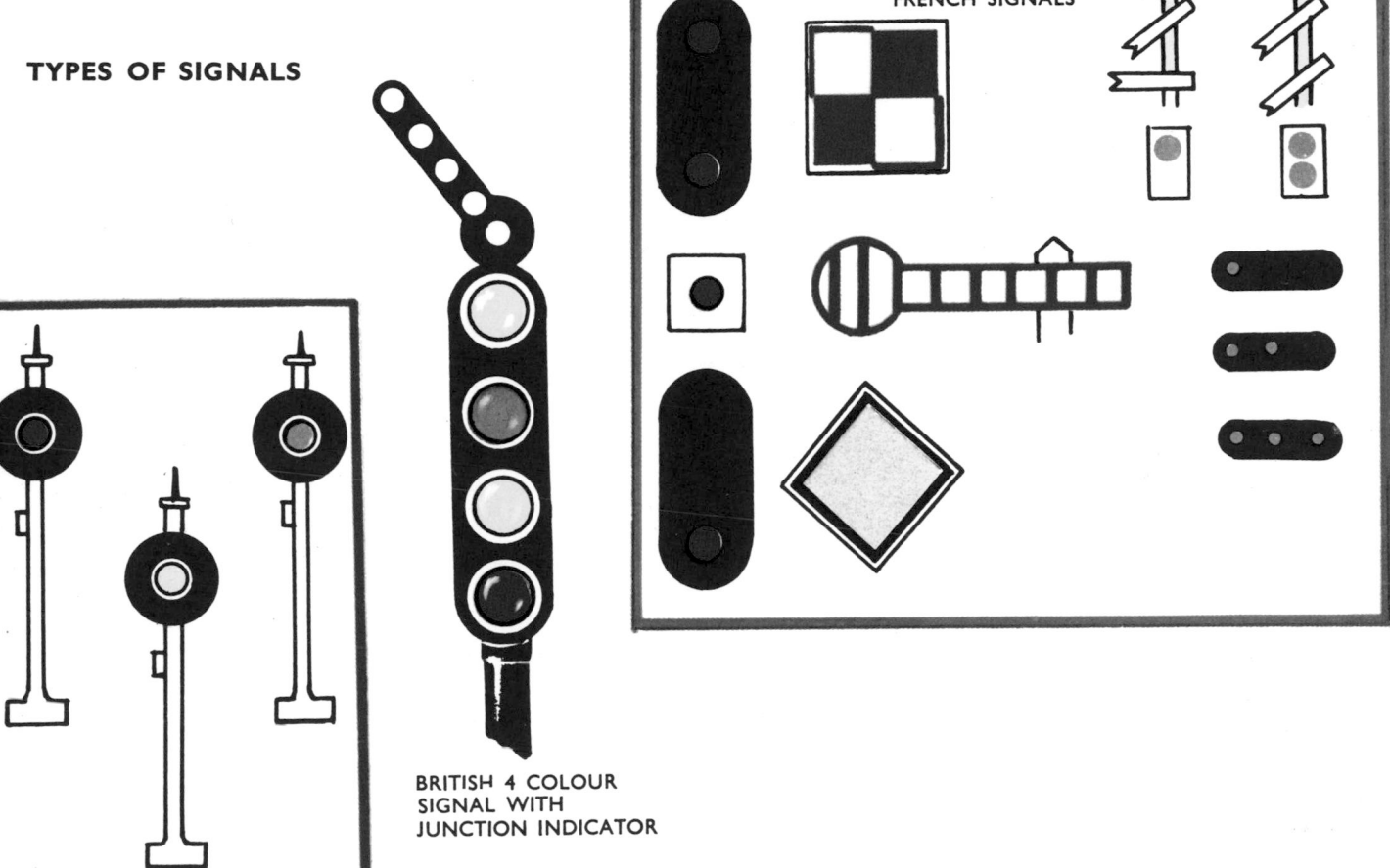

FRENCH SIGNALS

BRITISH 4 COLOUR
SIGNAL WITH
JUNCTION INDICATOR

AMERICAN SEARCHLIGHT SIGNAL

gradually they developed into a semaphore signal, which has a horizontal arm to show danger. The arm can be raised (or sometimes lowered) to show that the track is clear. Stop signals in Britain have square ends to the arms and must be obeyed, but there are also distant signals with fish-tail ends to the arms;

workers still refer to signals as "boards". Many semaphore signals and associated points can be worked from a single manual signal box, but there is a limit to the distance over which manual control by mechanical means is possible.

The invention of the electric needle telegraph by Cooke and Wheatstone in

1837 enabled the signalman, as he had by now become, to be told in advance what trains were on the way to him.

Although semaphore signals are very reliable and are still used in many parts of the world, the busiest modern lines have coloured light signalling, based on the night colours of the semaphores. Bright electric lamps are used with lenses which concentrate the light into a tight beam which can be seen for a long way even in daylight. Coloured light signals can have two, three or four aspects, the most common being three-aspect. In this case each signal is a stop signal but is also a distant signal for the one ahead. The three aspects are red, yellow and green; red meaning, as always, "danger—stop", yellow meaning "caution—be prepared to stop at the next signal if at red" and green giving the usual clear aspect.

On open track, away from stations and junctions, these signals are usually controlled by the trains themselves through track circuits. For track circuiting, the line is divided into sections insulated from one another and a low-voltage electric current is passed through one rail along the section and back through the other rail, making a circuit. At the end furthest from the current supply the connection between the rails is made through an electro-magnet which is energised by the current and holds a relay switch in place. When a train enters the section, the current takes the easier and shorter path through the train wheels and axles, the electro-magnet is de-energised and the relay switch drops. This switching action can be used to control other relays to produce a number of effects, one of which can be the placing

to danger of the signal controlling the section of track "in rear" of the train and the placing to caution of the signal for the section in rear of that. As the train proceeds, the signals automatically change to danger, caution and clear behind it, always keeping a space between trains.

The space between trains, or space interval in which only one train is allowed in one section at one time, distinguishes the modern from the early types of signalling, which were based on having a time interval. At busy points, approaches to stations, etc., it may be necessary to have trains closer together, and four-aspect signals may be used. These have an aspect showing two yellow lights, meaning that the next signal ahead will be at yellow. Another device is speed control signalling, to allow close approach to a station platform while another train is still there. In this case several signals are provided in conjunction with train speed measuring devices. The first signal will show red until the train speed has been reduced to, say, 30 m.p.h., the second until the speed is down to 25 m.p.h. and so on. By this means, as the distances between the train and the one ahead lessens, the speed is reduced to make sure the approaching train can stop safely if required.

Modern signalling puts very large areas under the control of one signal box, the positions of all trains being shown on a large illuminated diagram. Points and signals can be controlled from miles away by switches or push-buttons, often mounted on the diagram itself. A route can be set up through a maze of tracks simply by turning switches at the begin-

The interior of a modern signal box

ning and end of the selected route. The London Transport Underground system has developed programme machines which carry the whole day's timetable in the form of punched holes in a plastic roll. The roll moves forward under the control of a timing device and at the right times changes points and signals for the next train. The machines are supervised from a central point and the supervisor can operate any of the points and signals remotely by push-button if necessary.

Signalling is on the verge of a revolution in methods and already there are pointers to possible developments. One, for long stretches of open line, is a track radar which will probe ahead of the train and give warning of any obstruction. Linked to the rails, it will make it possible for drivers to see round corners. The other, perhaps more important, is the control of the signalling of a whole area by a computer which will know exactly where every train is and will issue instructions to each train to start, speed up, slow down, or stop, automatically. A one-man crew will be needed only to keep a look-out and take over in the event of failure of equipment.

Automatic train operation is already being tried by city railways, notably in Barcelona, New York, Moscow, Leningrad and London, though experiments are also in progress elsewhere.

New Projects

Railways are always trying new methods or improving old ones. One important new project—the new Tokaido line in Japan—is already running and marks the beginning of a new railway age. It has been built for high speeds, with a track separated from that of any other railway and without road level crossings, with control of its trains from a central point, and with only a few stations. Most railways in Japan have the 3 ft. 6 in. gauge, but this is 4 ft. 8½ in. Built in five years, the 322-mile line uses electric multiple-

29

unit trains to cover the whole distance, between Tokyo and Osaka, in three hours. The trains run on long-welded rails carried on concrete sleepers laid in crushed stone ballast, and collect electrical power at 25 kV. 60 cycles from an overhead system. Each pair of cars has its own silicon rectifier to convert the power supply to direct current for the four 170 kw. motors of each car. Nothing about the Tokaido line is revolutionary in itself. What *is* new is putting modern developments together in a completely new line built for the purpose.

The success of the line, opened in 1964, caused a new surge of interest in high-speed railways. The challenge was taken up in the United States and in Germany. A year later Germany had electric locomotives and trains capable of running at 125 m.p.h. and had begun bringing trunk railway routes up to a standard at which these speeds are possible. In the United States some remarkable designs have been produced for electric trains able to run up and down the North-East Corridor (Boston–New York–Washington) at speeds of 125–150 m.p.h. and Government help has been promised.

Channel Tunnel

Railways have to be planned to run where people (and goods) want to go, so that natural obstacles have to be overcome by bridges, embankments, cuttings and tunnels. One tunnel projected since at least 1802 would be built under the Channel so that trains could run from Britain to France and the rest of Europe, the Near East, and—with changes of bogies—even to the Pacific coast of Russia and China. The 1802 tunnel

30

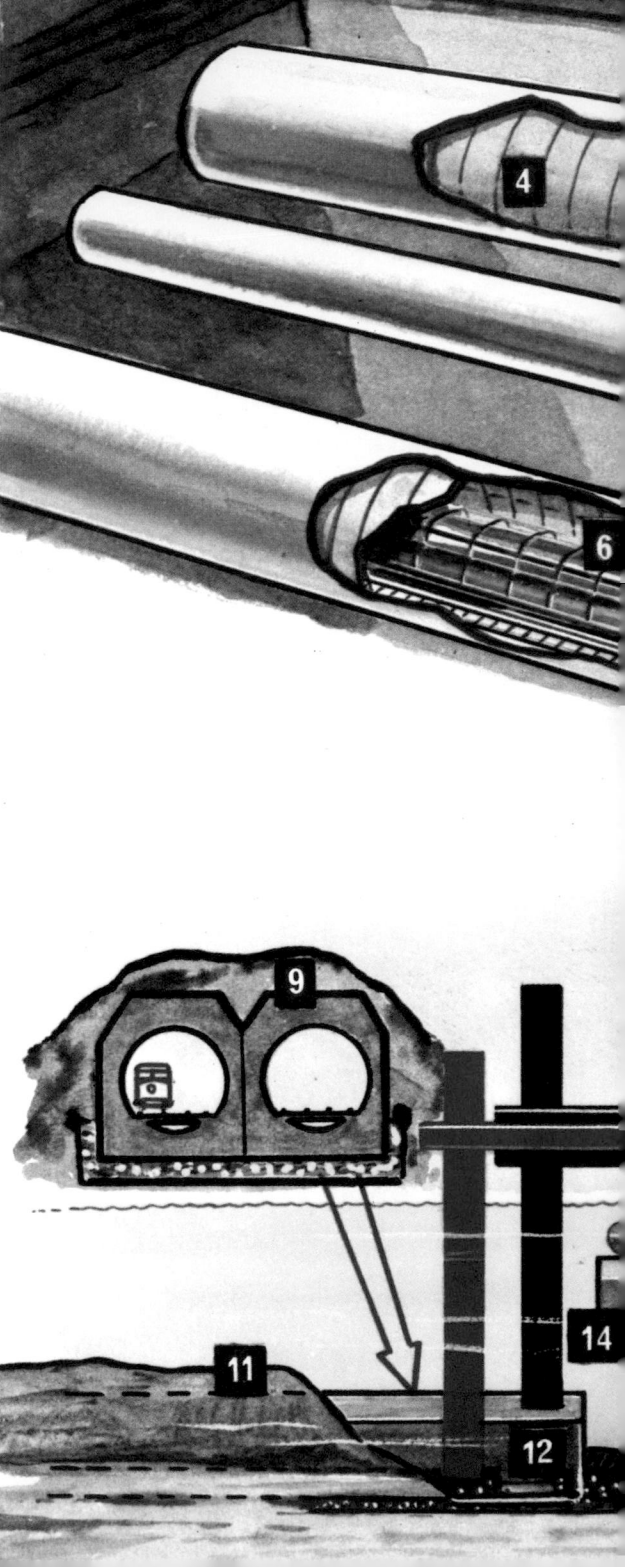

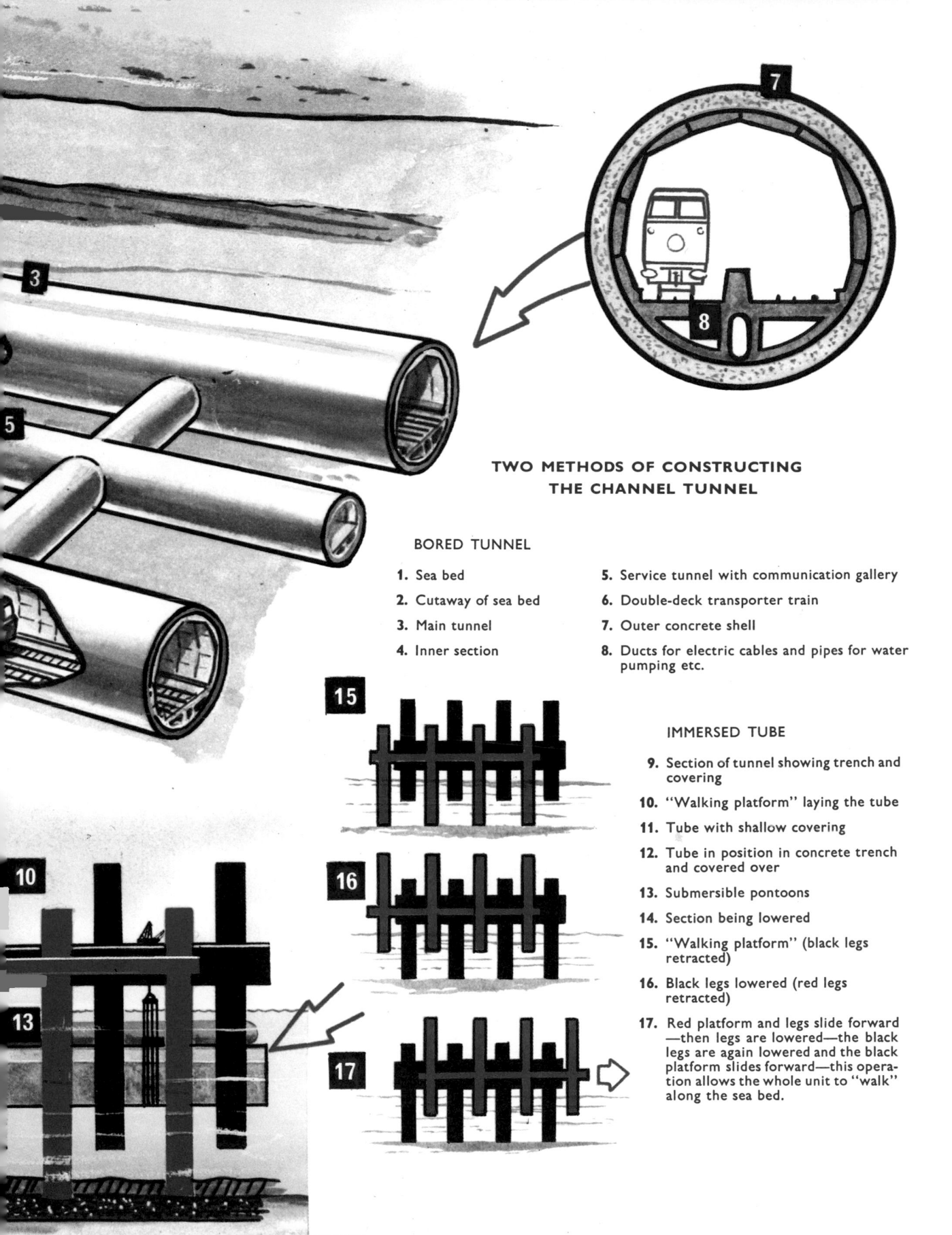

TWO METHODS OF CONSTRUCTING THE CHANNEL TUNNEL

BORED TUNNEL

1. Sea bed
2. Cutaway of sea bed
3. Main tunnel
4. Inner section
5. Service tunnel with communication gallery
6. Double-deck transporter train
7. Outer concrete shell
8. Ducts for electric cables and pipes for water pumping etc.

IMMERSED TUBE

9. Section of tunnel showing trench and covering
10. "Walking platform" laying the tube
11. Tube with shallow covering
12. Tube in position in concrete trench and covered over
13. Submersible pontoons
14. Section being lowered
15. "Walking platform" (black legs retracted)
16. Black legs lowered (red legs retracted)
17. Red platform and legs slide forward —then legs are lowered—the black legs are again lowered and the black platform slides forward—this operation allows the whole unit to "walk" along the sea bed.

would have been for road traffic, with an artificial island in the middle of the Channel so that the horses could come up to rest, but a railway tunnel had been worked out in detail by 1857 by Thomas de Gamond. The scheme took on practical shape with the formation of the Channel Tunnel Company in 1872 and the beginning of a pilot bore in 1880. The pilot tunnel was $1\frac{1}{3}$ miles long. Two years later a similar pilot tunnel was started on the French side and was continued for $1\frac{1}{4}$ miles. The tunnels are still there.

Many studies were undertaken through the years, but a Channel Tunnel Study Group with British, French and American members began work in 1957 and reported in 1959. The group considered a rail tunnel, a road tunnel, a combined road/rail tunnel, and a bridge (first proposed in 1836). They favoured a rail tunnel to be operated jointly by French and British Railways. The prospects for the tunnel, which has the blessing in principle of the British and French Governments, seem good.

One scheme is for two single-track tunnels side-by-side, each about 21 ft. 6 in. in diameter. Between them, and with connecting passages to them, will run another, smaller service tunnel for maintenance, drainage, ventilation and so on. The trains will be hauled by electric locomotives. Speeds of nearly 90 m.p.h. and train intervals of no more than 3 minutes are expected.

There will be a special shuttle service for road vehicles with terminals at Frethun on the French side and at a site on the London–Dover railway on the British side. The distance between them would be 42 miles, of which 32 miles would be in tunnel and 22 miles under the Channel. The tunnel would cross the coastlines near Dover and Calais.

The road vehicles—150 cars, trucks and coaches per train—will drive on to trains of flat wagons. For peak periods, double-deck trains holding 300 cars will be available. The passengers will normally remain in their cars for the 45 minute trip. Up to 12 road vehicle trains an hour will be run if required—there will be no waiting—and three through passenger or freight trains an hour will be needed.

A $4\frac{1}{2}$-hour train journey from the centre of London to the centre of Paris will be a strong challenge to the airlines, whose passengers face a long airport–city centre journey at each end of the flight.

Railways of the Future

In the future, many railway systems are likely to be pruned until only a few lines remain, but these will be of a very high standard. The track will be of steel rails welded end-to-end, to make the passage of trains quiet and smooth. Trains will be driven automatically by orders sent to them along the track by a computer housed in a central control. Passenger trains will probably continue to carry one man to take charge if there is a breakdown and to give assurance to passengers, but freight trains will be crewless. Coaches and wagons will be very large compared with those of today and, because there will be fewer lines, with one route running between major cities instead of the two or three routes of today, it will pay to enlarge tunnels so that these bigger vehicles can be used.

Freight will be carried in containers,

Transport experts all over the world are trying to find a solution to the problem of moving vast numbers of people through cities and towns. This picture shows a possible answer. An underground railway helps to carry people who would otherwise have to crowd into cars and buses. At the same time more people would travel in safe and efficient monorail coaches high above the city streets. A transport network such as this might become a common sight in the future.

including convertible road/rail vehicles. There will be mechanised depots of the sort now used in the United States and under construction in Britain for liner trains where containers will be transferred. Such depots need only a small staff. Wagons will be sorted quickly and automatically in mechanised marshalling yards using further developments of today's techniques. The central control will allow more use to be made of the track capacity of the main lines, so it will be possible to run shorter, but more frequent, trains.

Train speeds, especially if the linear electric motor is developed, may go up to 200 m.p.h. or even more. Possibly, in time, the track itself will change. The train of the next century may have no wheels, only air cushions which will enable it to hover an inch or two above a concrete track along which it will be hurled by a linear motor. With such a motor, a train can be braked by reversing the current, so that friction, both the ally and enemy of the railway engineer, will be conquered at last.

SOME OF THE WORLD'S FAMOUS PASSENGER TRAINS

Above: The Italian Settebello

Left: The Trans European Express

Below: The Cross-Channel Night Ferry

Above: The North American Empire Builder

Left: The Japanese Tokaido Line

Below: The Flying Scotsman.

ROAD TRANSPORT

Roads are probably man's oldest transport medium. The primitive hunter must have dragged his kills back to the winter cave by routes which in time became defined paths. His wanderings probably followed the trails of the animal herds and hardened into fixed routes which became tracks. It was the primitive track which beckoned man and his pack-animals to explore the nearer world.

The basic purpose of a road is that it should lead from one established place to another by the easiest route. The easiest way is not always the nearest. Roads wind up the sides of mountains and along the slopes of valleys, taking many miles to cover quite a short distance—but only a mountain goat could take the shortest route.

Roads did not become a matter of engineering until wheeled transport

Three-level freeways in San Francisco, U.S.A.

reached an advanced stage. The Babylonians had paved roads in 2000 B.C., but road building came to perfection with the Romans. All over Europe the Romans built their roads, running straight from fort to fort or garrison town to garrison town—for they were built for military use. They used smoke from signal fires to lay out a straight line, and the roads proceed up hill and down dale with few deviations. Where they did change direction, it was usually on a hill-top where signal fires from both directions could be sighted. These roads were accurately surveyed and properly drained to keep the stone foundations free from water. Along these superb paths passed the legions and the wheeled traffic of the Roman Empire.

What Roads are Made of

After the fall of Rome, the ordered way of life needed for engineering feats of this kind fell apart and roads deteriorated again to mud tracks. It was not until mechanical transport came on the scene that there was any incentive to spend money on roads again. Famous among the early eighteenth century road engincers are Thomas Telford and James Loudon Macadam, both of whom used heavy stone foundations on which was a layer of lighter, smaller stone and a top surface of small or crushed stone. Nowadays such roads are sealed with tar, often as a component of a tar (or bitumen) and small stone surfacing rolled in with a heavy roller.

Another popular road material is concrete, laid in large slabs half the width of the road and up to 20 ft. long. These are up to 12 in. thick and the joints between slabs are sealed with a bitumen compound which allows a certain amount of expansion and contraction. On busy stretches such roads have a bitumen-based top dressing. Roads are cambered to let surface water run off to the sides, though the most modern roads tend to have a camber so reduced as to be almost unnoticeable.

Great advances have been made in producing surfaces which tend to reduce the likelihood of skidding by vehicles, and some short sections where a bad surface would cause great delays have electric heating elements incorporated so that ice and snow can be melted before they can settle.

Steam Carriage and Motor Car

The first steam road carriage, invented by Nicolas Cugnot, appeared in France in 1769 and a larger version carried passengers along a public street in 1770, but it was the invention of the internal-combustion engine which really began the process which has flooded the roads of the world with vehicles. This is not because steam carriages were unsuccessful. Gurney, the first man to build a mechanically-propelled vehicle with fare-paying passengers, was carrying people between London and Bath in 1827. Four years later some of his coaches were running a regular Gloucester–Cheltenham service at an average speed of 12 m.p.h. Hancock's steam omnibuses of this period in the London area were also very successful and coaches built by William Church ran between London and Birmingham for a few years from 1832. Great Britain might have had the reputation for steam road vehicles that it had for railways had

not the turnpike authorities who maintained some main roads, collecting tolls to pay for the work, charged 12 times as much for steam coaches as for a four-in-hand coach. The Highways Act of 1865 aided the work of suppression by making it compulsory for a man on foot, carrying a red flag, to walk 100 yards in front of mechanically propelled vehicles, which were not supposed to exceed 4 m.p.h.

Early cars

The Highways Act is important because it also impeded the early motor car in Great Britain. Probably the first petrol-engined car was built by Siegfried Markus of Vienna in the 1870s, but few details are known. The inventors best known are the Germans Karl Benz and Gottlieb Daimler. The first Benz car, a three-wheeler, made its first trip in 1885 and reached $7\frac{1}{2}$ m.p.h. Edward Butler, in Britain, built, quite independently, a petrol tricycle in 1888 and followed it up with improved versions. Benjamin Jacobs produced an oil-engined four-wheel car and displayed it in 1886, but the British pioneers, disheartened by the Highways Act, gave up. The first Daimler car appeared in 1886, and in 1889 Daimler and his colleague Wilhelm Maybach produced a car with a water-cooled engine, a four-speed gearbox, and a tubular radiator, laying the foundation of modern motor car practice.

In 1879 the American George Seldon, sometimes regarded as the father of the motor car, had applied for a patent for a motor car which had most of the features of the European cars, but he delayed actually taking the patent out until 1895. From the beginning of the present century improvement was rapid—even in Britain where the red flag and 4 m.p.h. limitation was withdrawn in 1896 and other restrictions in 1903. In France, Panhard and Levassor built a car in 1894 to Daimler patents and reached 15 m.p.h. By 1899 a 16 h.p. car by the same builders won a 1,377-mile road race in France at an average of 30·8 m.p.h.

In the next few years many now famous names appeared in the motor car industry. Henry Ford, who had built his first car in 1892, began working on his own in 1902 and built two successful 80 h.p. racing cars in 1903. He formed the Ford Motor Company immediately the success of these cars had been demonstrated, and produced several types of car before concentrating on the famous model "T" in 1909. This was the car which popularised motoring, and by the beginning of the First World War, Henry Ford was

38

building 250,000 a year. Rolls-Royce, at the other end of the scale, began production in 1904, and in 1907 ran an officially-observed reliability trial with a 40/50 h.p. "Silver Ghost". The car ran for 14,377 miles without mechanical troubles and was then examined for wear. The repair bill was 40 shillings.

Speed Records

On Daytona Beach, in 1927, Major Segrave raised the world's speed record to 203·79 m.p.h. with a 1,000 h.p. Sunbeam. Two years later he brought it to 231·46 m.p.h. The saga was carried on by Sir Malcolm Campbell, who raised the record nearly every year, reaching 301·13 m.p.h. in 1935. In 1937 Captain George Eyston brought it to 312·2 m.p.h. and in 1938 to 357·5 m.p.h. John Cobb took up the challenge, reaching 369 m.p.h. in 1939 and 394·1 m.p.h. in 1947. This figure stood until 1964, when Donald Campbell in a jet-powered car achieved 403 m.p.h. at Lake Eyre in Australia. The fastest land speed of all in anything resembling a car was the 526·26 m.p.h. of Craig Breedlove, an American, in 1964. He used a three-wheel jet-propelled vehicle which did not qualify for the land speed record—the regulations specify four wheels.

Breedlove's "car" was not so much a car as a wingless jet plane. The main virtue of racing is that new ideas can be tried out and new components tested to the utmost under the worst, most severe conditions. Lessons learned in racing have contributed to making the family car the easily driven, reliable machine it is today. (The fastest land vehicles travel on rails. Their performance is secret but it is known that top speeds are about 2,000 m.p.h. They are rocket sledges used by the U.S. Navy for testing aircraft and missile components under controlled conditions. The fastest man in the world, on land, may have ridden, in secret, on such a sledge.)

Cars and Trucks

Private motor cars vary tremendously in size, tiny machines being found in France and monsters developing 330–350 h.p. in the U.S.A. Examples of these extremes are the Citroen Bijou with a 425 c.c. engine and a top speed of under 45 m.p.h. compared with the Chevrolet Corvette Sting Ray, which has a 5,360 c.c. engine and can approach 150 m.p.h. The normal family car in Europe tends to have an engine of between 1,000 and 2,000 c.c. capacity, to seat four or five people, to be capable of 70–85 m.p.h. and

39

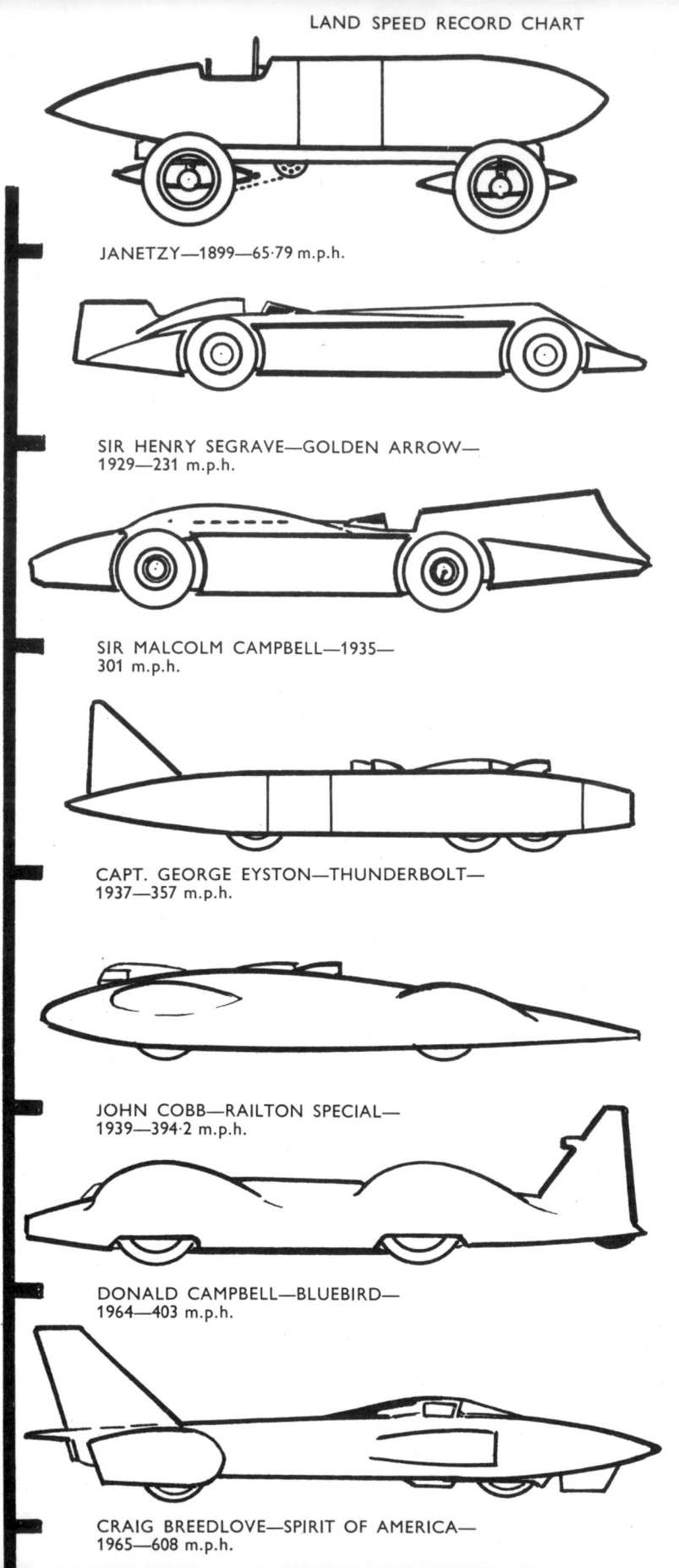

JANETZY—1899—65·79 m.p.h.

SIR HENRY SEGRAVE—GOLDEN ARROW—
1929—231 m.p.h.

SIR MALCOLM CAMPBELL—1935—
301 m.p.h.

CAPT. GEORGE EYSTON—THUNDERBOLT—
1937—357 m.p.h.

JOHN COBB—RAILTON SPECIAL—
1939—394·2 m.p.h.

DONALD CAMPBELL—BLUEBIRD—
1964—403 m.p.h.

CRAIG BREEDLOVE—SPIRIT OF AMERICA—
1965—608 m.p.h.

to be able to run at least 60,000 miles before any really expensive repairs are likely to be needed. American cars are usually larger and faster as befits the greater distances and the American habit of using cars instead of trains on long journeys (if they are not flying).

The story of commercial vehicles is very similar to that of private motor cars and depended on the same technical developments. The tendency in recent years has been for light trucks to follow the motor car, often using the same chassis and engine and having the same sort of performance, and for heavier vehicles to have diesel engines, to grow larger, and to develop power aids to driving. Different-purpose bodies can be supplied to fit a single chassis and the performance of a basic unit can be varied by semi-articulation, in which the engine and cab are fitted to a short chassis with a massive rear wheel assembly. The freight is carried on a special form of semi-trailer, which has rear wheels only. The front of the trailer is attached to the rear of the powered vehicle, or tractor, by one of several types of automatic coupling. The tractor can perform other work while a trailer is being loaded or unloaded.

To limit the load on the road, most countries impose a restriction on the weight carried per wheel or axle, so that larger trucks often have two axles at the rear and sometimes have two, both steering, at the front. Special vehicles for heavy loads—usually designed with particular loads in mind—may have many axles and even means of steering the trailer axles. In Europe, on long-distance routes, two or even three trailers may be hitched behind a powerful lorry to make up a "road train". Single European vehicles are up to 36 ft. long, but in the United States 40 ft. is not unusual. Vehicle combinations may be considerably longer.

The ordinary car or truck is often fitted nowadays with equipment which formerly would have been kept for expensive or specialised vehicles. One of these items is automatic transmission, which does away with the clutch pedal, leaving accelerator and brake only. The vehicle is fitted with devices which measure the road speed, the demands of the load, and the position of the accelerator, and engage the appropriate gear. A fluid flywheel or similar device enables the vehicle to stand still while the engine is idling. When the driver releases the brake and presses the accelerator the automatic control engages bottom gear and the other gears in succession as the speed rises. When the brakes are applied the gears are shifted down again as speed falls. When the load on the engine grows as a hill is climbed the gears are changed down again. Lower gears can be held for quick acceleration, or when the driver wants to use his engine as a brake on a long hill.

Most vehicles have the type of brake which expands composition shoes against the inside of a brake drum. Under heavy duty conditions, this type of brake can "fade", especially when hot or wet, and high performance cars and many freight vehicles use disc brakes. These consist of discs of metal arranged to spin with the wheels and to be gripped between jaws when the brakes are applied.

Large vehicles and some heavy motor cars have power assisted steering, the usual arrangement being that the movement of the steering wheel brings servo-mechanisms into play which give a push in the required direction. This is a great help to the driver when parking or manoeuvring at low speeds.

Car and Truck Motors

Both petrol motors and diesel motors have become lighter and more efficient, extra power coming mainly from higher revolutions per minute. Diesel motors may turn at 2,000–3,000 r.p.m. and petrol motors at 5,000–6,000 r.p.m., but some petrol motors may run up to considerably higher speeds than this.

Conventional motors have a large number of moving parts, limiting the speed at which they can be run. Efforts to find a simpler type of motor have been in progress for many years, and, following in the steps of the steam engine builders, designers turned to turbines. The principle of such turbines is that fuel is burnt to form gas which is directed into a turbine to turn the blades and produce power. Experimental versions, include one by the British Rover Company which did well in the 1964 Le Mans 24-hour competition. An experimental gas-turbine-powered road train, weighing more than 75 tons, was shown in 1964 by the Ford Company in the U.S.A. It consists of a three-axle tractor with a 600 h.p. turbine hauling two semi-trailers each 40 ft. long. It has a fuel range of up to 600 miles, and also air-conditioning and other refinements for crew comfort. The off-duty driver can turn his seat into a bed, or can watch television on a small screen out of the driver's line of sight. There is a cooker, sink, refrigerator, toilet and

A rear view of the Rover-B.R.M. Gas Turbine car. The principle of such turbines is that fuel is burnt to form gas which is directed into a turbine to turn the blades and produce power.

Another view of the Rover-B.R.M. A prize of £5,000 was offered to the first gas turbine car to complete the 24 hours Le Mans race which this car won, finishing third, in 1964.

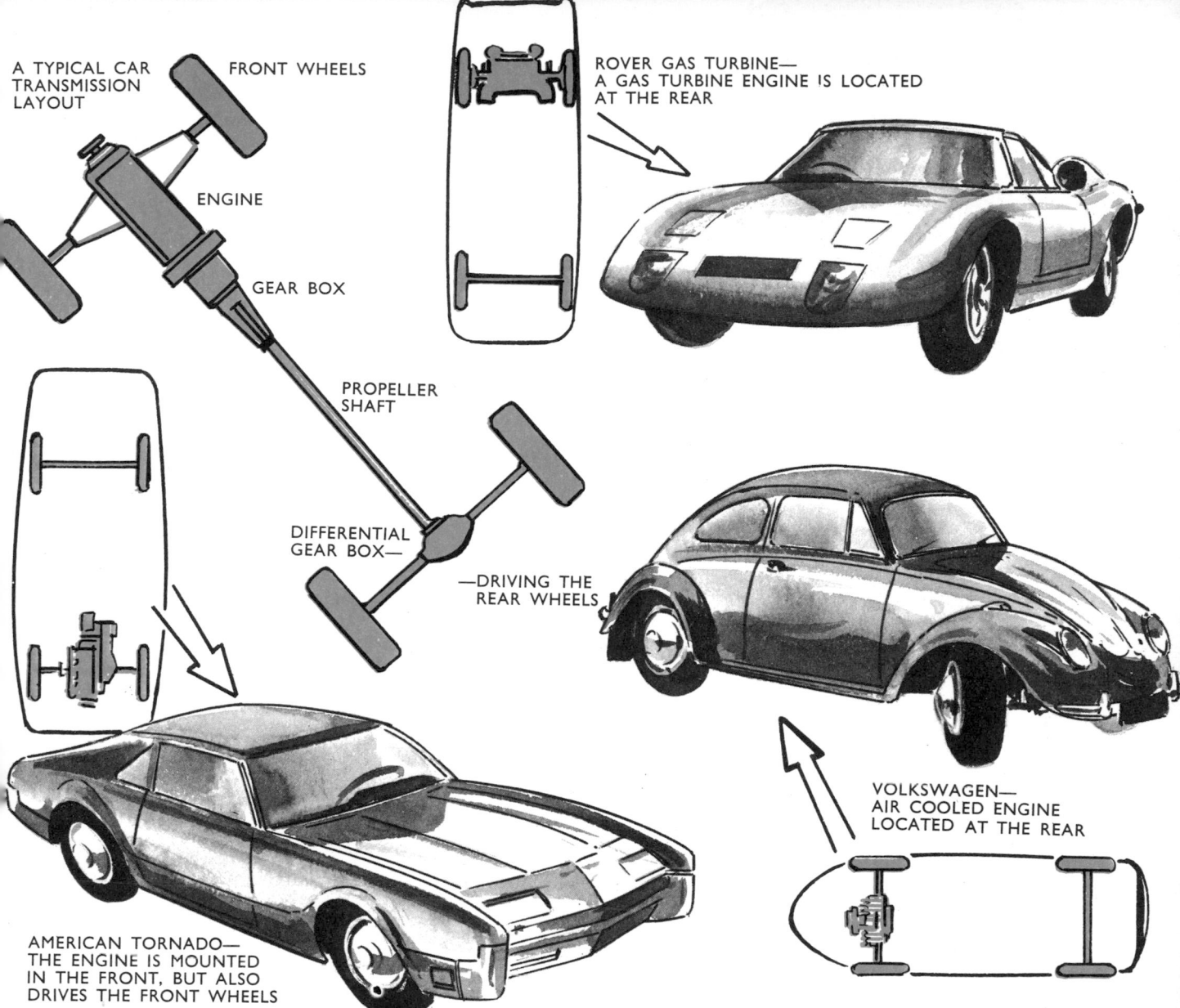

A TYPICAL CAR TRANSMISSION LAYOUT

FRONT WHEELS

ENGINE

GEAR BOX

PROPELLER SHAFT

DIFFERENTIAL GEAR BOX—

—DRIVING THE REAR WHEELS

ROVER GAS TURBINE— A GAS TURBINE ENGINE IS LOCATED AT THE REAR

VOLKSWAGEN— AIR COOLED ENGINE LOCATED AT THE REAR

AMERICAN TORNADO— THE ENGINE IS MOUNTED IN THE FRONT, BUT ALSO DRIVES THE FRONT WHEELS

CAR TRANSMISSION LAY-OUTS

radio as well as television.

Showing great promise is the Wankel engine, which uses a rotating member instead of cylinders to receive the power of the exploding fuel. The few moving parts make this a simple and potentially cheap and easily maintained engine. Another development, at present mainly for the armed forces, is the multi-fuel engine which will run on practically anything from high-octane petrol to diesel fuel and paraffin.

Public Transport

Public transport—apart from railways —consists of trams, trolley buses and

43

motor buses. Buses, drawn by horses, were the first to arrive, though passenger coaches and carts went back long before the first vehicles to be called omnibuses appeared in Paris in 1828. Something similar had already run in Paris in 1819 with a flat fare of five sous. London's first omnibus was introduced by George Shillibeer in 1829 and New York's by John Stephenson in 1831.

The first street car or tram appeared in New York in 1832, and the first electric street car in 1884 at Kansas City. A Dr. Finney in the United States produced drawings of a trolley bus in 1882, though it was never built, and Siemens & Halske in Germany produced, at about the same time, a road vehicle drawn by a small carriage containing an electric motor running on two overhead wires. The trolley vehicle began to resemble its present form in France and America at the beginning of the present century.

Trams have almost vanished from the U.S.A. and Britain, but hold their place in European countries. Britain had many double-decked trams but in Europe generally single-deck trams with trailers were (and are) used. Some cities, such as Rotterdam, now have articulated trams—long, two-bodied vehicles with a special full-width turntable connection between them to make virtually one vehicle. They run on wheels which have rubber inserts to make them silent and avoid the familiar clanking and roaring of trams on tight curves.

Some early trams were worked by cables running in trenches down the middle of the road, the cars having grippers to connect them to or release them from the continuously-running cable as required. Andrew Hallidie first applied this principle to street cars in San Francisco in 1873, on Clay Street Hill—and gained a great success. The cable cars, as they were called, became so famous that they are now a national institution and are preserved as a memorial to the old days, while still continuing to move people about the city.

Trolley buses suffered from being intermediate vehicles combining characteristics of both trams and buses without having the full advantages of either. Though many were built and ran successfully for years, and there are still a fair number in various parts of the world, they are coming to the end of their life.

The omnibus, which grew through horse, steam, electric and petrol-motored versions to the almost universal diesel-motored vehicle of today, has the advantage of not being tied to overhead wires. It can be switched from route to route, or district to district, as the demand for transport changes. Most of the world's buses are single decked, but London has always had great numbers of double-deck vehicles. Some European cities, and others like New York, have had double deck vehicles at times and there are signs that this type of bus may enjoy a revival. There are, for example. double-deck buses 36 ft. long in Stockholm worked by one man. One-man-operation of buses is becoming the rule in the drive to reduce costs and provide cheap public transport. Even a large vehicle can be worked by one man when a flat fare—one price for any distance—is in operation. The passenger can buy tokens or tickets in advance, slip a coin into a turnstile as he enters the bus, or pay the driver.

New Ford project with 12 headlights each of 1 inch diameter and light strip along body.

LIGHT STRIP

12 HEADLIGHTS

INTERIOR OF CAR

Undertakings that charge according to distance travelled have a much more difficult problem. Drivers can take fares on reasonably-sized vehicles on not-too-busy routes, but it is impossible on busy routes with large vehicles holding 70 or 80 people. One possibility is that the upper decks of double-deck buses could be closed outside the rush hour period so that one man could deal with the smaller number of passengers carried on the lower deck.

An alternative to double-deck buses is the bus with trailer. In Budapest, buses with two trailers may be seen, and articulated buses like the street cars already described are spreading to European cities.

A form of passenger road transport not yet mentioned is the coach—really a bus with a more luxurious body. Many coaches are used for pleasure excursions, but some undertake long-distance regular runs which, like the Greyhound network in the U.S.A., may span whole contin-ents. On good roads coaches such as these can run at up to 80 m.p.h. and could compete with trains if they were not slowed down greatly at the approaches to city centres. Long-distance coaches may have refreshment facilities like those of aircraft, toilets and bars, and carry a hostess. London has a service of limited stop coaches—Green Line coaches—which radiate out to serve districts within about 30 miles of the capital.

Not strictly a public service vehicle, but important all the same, is the school bus. These are especially noticeable in the United States, where driving the bright yellow vehicles, seating 40 or more, is often a part-time job for housewives.

Trucks and Freight Handling

Trucks can be fitted with special bodies suitable for almost any form of traffic and with apparatus to handle the goods they carry, using hydraulic power from the engine. Typical is the tipping lorry, the body of which can be lifted at the front by a hydraulic ram so that the load slides out at the back. They can also be tipped to either side and are used mainly for carrying sand and gravel. Other lorries are fitted with tail hoists—hydraulic powered platforms which raise heavy items from ground level to the level of the lorry floor. Some lorries have hydraulic cranes to lift heavy objects on and off. A new method of delivering coal and other solid fuels is by means of a semi-trailer with a hopper body which can be loaded from above and can unload itself by built-in conveyor belts.

Some ingenious machines have been evolved for transport in factories. One of the most useful is the fork-lift truck, ranging in capacity from a few hundred-weight to many tons. This type of truck has a vertical slide at the front from which projects a fork-shaped arm. The fork is powered by a hydraulic ram which can raise or lower it as required. These trucks usually work with pallets (small load-bearing platforms on which goods are piled for storage or removal) or containers, both of which have openings suitable for receiving the forks. The truck is driven up to the load with the slide upright, and the two prongs of the fork are inserted into the openings. The slide is then tilted back, raising the load slightly and ensuring that it is secure on the fork. The truck then carries the load

46

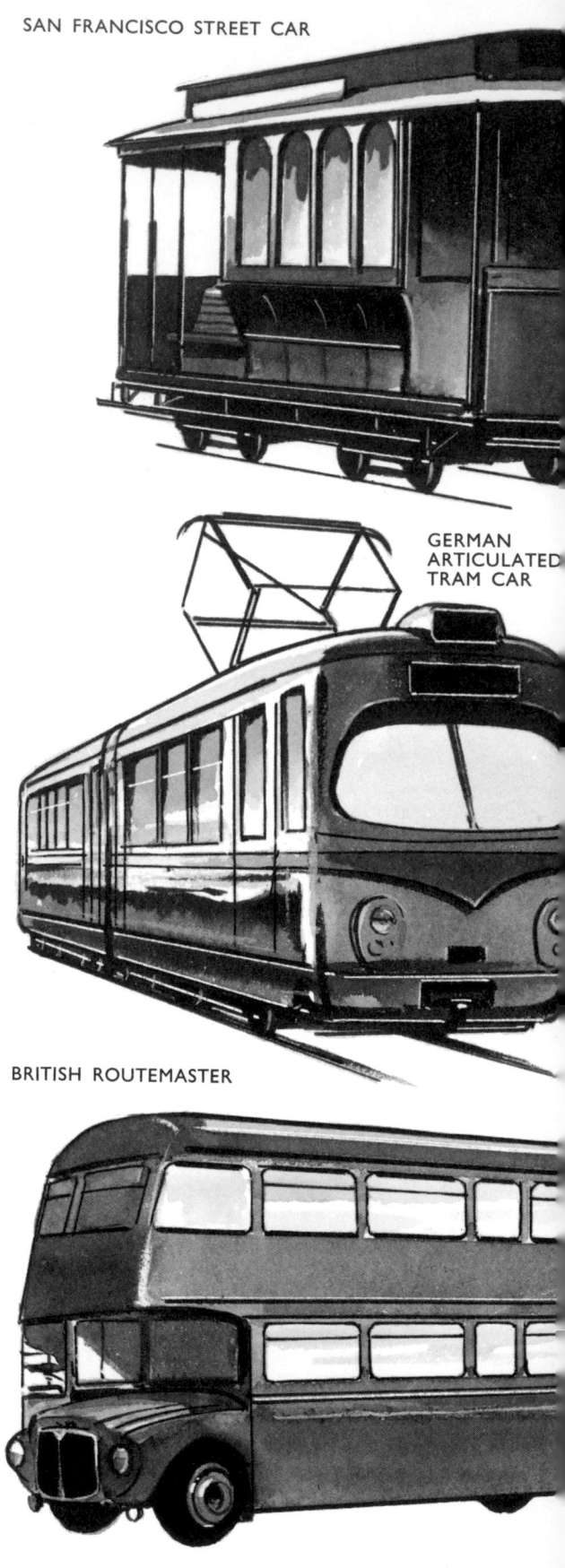

GERMAN ARTICULATED TRAM CAR

BRITISH ROUTEMASTER

GERMAN OMNIBUS

HUNGARIAN ARTICULATED BUS

AMERICAN HIGH SPEED COACH

off to wherever it is required. The slide makes it possible to lift the load to the level of a lorry or wagon floor.

Pallets, containers and similar systems are of increasing importance in enabling loads to be transferred from one form of transport to another. There are international standards for pallets and containers. Pallets of one size—32 in. × 48 in.—are available in an international pool. Containers can be large or of a small intermediate type for bulk goods, carrying 20–40 cwt. These can be rigid, carrying solids or liquids, or in the form of rubber or nylon bags, or even of corrugated paper. These last can be thrown away after use. As well as fork-lift trucks, side-loaders are often used for handling this type of container. This machine picks up and carries a load along its side and it is particularly suitable for long loads which must be loaded lengthwise. For timber and other very long items a straddle loader is sometimes used. This is a powerful truck with its wheels on long legs, giving a large amount of room under the truck body. The straddle truck runs astride a load of timber, hoists it beneath its body, and takes it away. Big mobile gantry cranes are used to transfer containers from lorry to wagon and back at some railway terminals, the gantries being wide enough to span road and siding at one time.

Some trailers capable of being transferred between road and rail were mentioned earlier, but another one popular in the United States is the Flexivan, which, when fitted with a two-axle bogie, makes a 40 ft. road semi-trailer. It can also be rail "Piggy-backed". Without the wheels it can be divided into two 20 ft.

48

containers for carriage by rail or sea.

Largely because many of the short sea-route ships in Europe are railway-owned and run from railway-owned or financed ports, co-operation between rail and sea travel on routes about European shores is good. Most docks of any size are rail-served and were designed from the first with rail wagon/ship transfer in mind. Trucks often have to travel through congested areas to get to the docks and there is not always a great deal of room for them when they get there, especially when railway sheds and lines bar the way. The more modern docks are being built with road transport in mind as well as the traditional rail.

In latter years, as a result of experience with tank landing craft during the war, a few services have grown up in which ships of this type are used to carry laden trucks across sea barriers from country to country. The trucks run aboard along a ramp through nose doors in the ship and are parked on a vehicle deck. In this way a truck loaded, say, in Northern Ireland, could carry goods all the way to a customer in Germany.

Cars accompanied by drivers and passengers can also be driven on to car ferries—most of them owned by the railways. There are also aircraft capable of

Modern Methods of moving freight

Left: A British Road Services container.

Below left: Road—Rail A British Railways container.

Below: Road—Sea A container is taken off a truck and loaded on to a ship.

ferrying two or three cars at a time over long distances. These are also built on the "drive-on, drive-off" principle.

Transfer of freight loads between rail or road vehicles and ships is normally by crane, the goods being placed on flat platforms or in nets to be lifted. There are now special container-carrying ships which take goods already packed in their containers, saving a great deal of time in loading or unloading. Ships can be designed with fittings enabling containers to be taken aboard and stowed in their proper place, deck by deck, by mechanical methods. Only a few men are needed to operate the system.

An Italian motorway, which is a toll road. Many countries pay for their motorways by charging the motorist as he drives on to it.

AUTOMATIC ROAD SYSTEM

WARNING
LIGHT ON

DETECTION LOOP

CONTROL

DETECTOR

A network of wires buried in the road controls the vehicle. The driver operates a switch on the dashboard which brings in an 'automatic driver' capable of steering, braking, accelerating and watching the road ahead. Mounted at each end of the car are tiny antennas connected to a radio inside the car which is linked to an electro-mechanical system controlling all the movements of the car. Control stations are spaced at five-mile intervals along the motorway cables. If the vehicle wanders from the centre lane pick-up cable, the signals controlling the car bring it back to the selected lane. The system also controls the speed and regulates the distance between each car. If the car is being driven manually the lights at the side of the road still serve to warn the driver if he is too close to the car ahead or if a crash has occured in front.

51

Roads and Highways

There are two basic problems with road transport. One is the best way to gain speed with safety on inter-city runs and the other is how to handle traffic when it gets to the city.

Motorways or highways enable traffic to move quickly from place to place, but joining or leaving them entails complicated systems of dive-unders and flyovers to ensure that vehicles enter or leave the proper traffic stream without crossing any other stream on the level. These requirements have led to the building of huge clover-leaf shaped junctions which sprawl over many acres of countryside. Where more than one road meets a motorway at the same point, the junctions become even more complicated.

To make allowances for human error, the total width of a motorway has to be wider than it need be if precise steering could be relied on and there were no overtaking. Alternatively, an existing road might carry four lanes of traffic instead of three. A suggestion which has been tried with success on a small scale is that cars should be driven automatically on highways. Each highway lane would have a buried cable down its centre which would emit constant impulses. Apparatus on the car would pick up the impulses and control the steering so that the car exactly straddled the cable. Within a few inches, the car would steer as accurately as if it were on rails. A refinement would also control the speed of the vehicle within narrow limits. With such a system, the driver would enter the motorway as he does now and align his car over a painted line in the roadway. Supposing that he picked the "blue" lane for 50 m.p.h., he would run the car astride the painted line, take the speed up to about 50 m.p.h. and then press a switch for the automatic control to take over. The car would then be steered, at the correct speed, as far as desired. The driver could read a book, talk, listen to the radio, or do anything else until he approached the point where he had to leave the motorway. Pressing another switch would shunt the car automatically on to a special leaving lane. When the painted line reappeared on the road surface the driver would take back control and drive off the motorway in the usual way. If the driver falls asleep, or for some other reason fails to take back control, the car is automatically brought to a halt, flashing lights and signs warning vehicles behind.

Modern techniques of motor road construction can carry through traffic in the city area by raised roads, crossing over streets, railways, houses and offices, or through tunnels diving under the busy city centre, but the large number of vehicles entering a city, especially in the morning peak hour, and leaving again in the evening is one of the most intractable problems. Counting devices can be arranged to illuminate signs which will switch traffic to another road when one is choked, and numbers of such devices can be linked to a computer which will automatically direct traffic over the clearest routes, but the main trouble is that there is nowhere for the vehicles to go when they arrive.

When all reasonable allowance for off-street parking has been made, and parking meters have made parking on the

TYPES OF BRIDGES

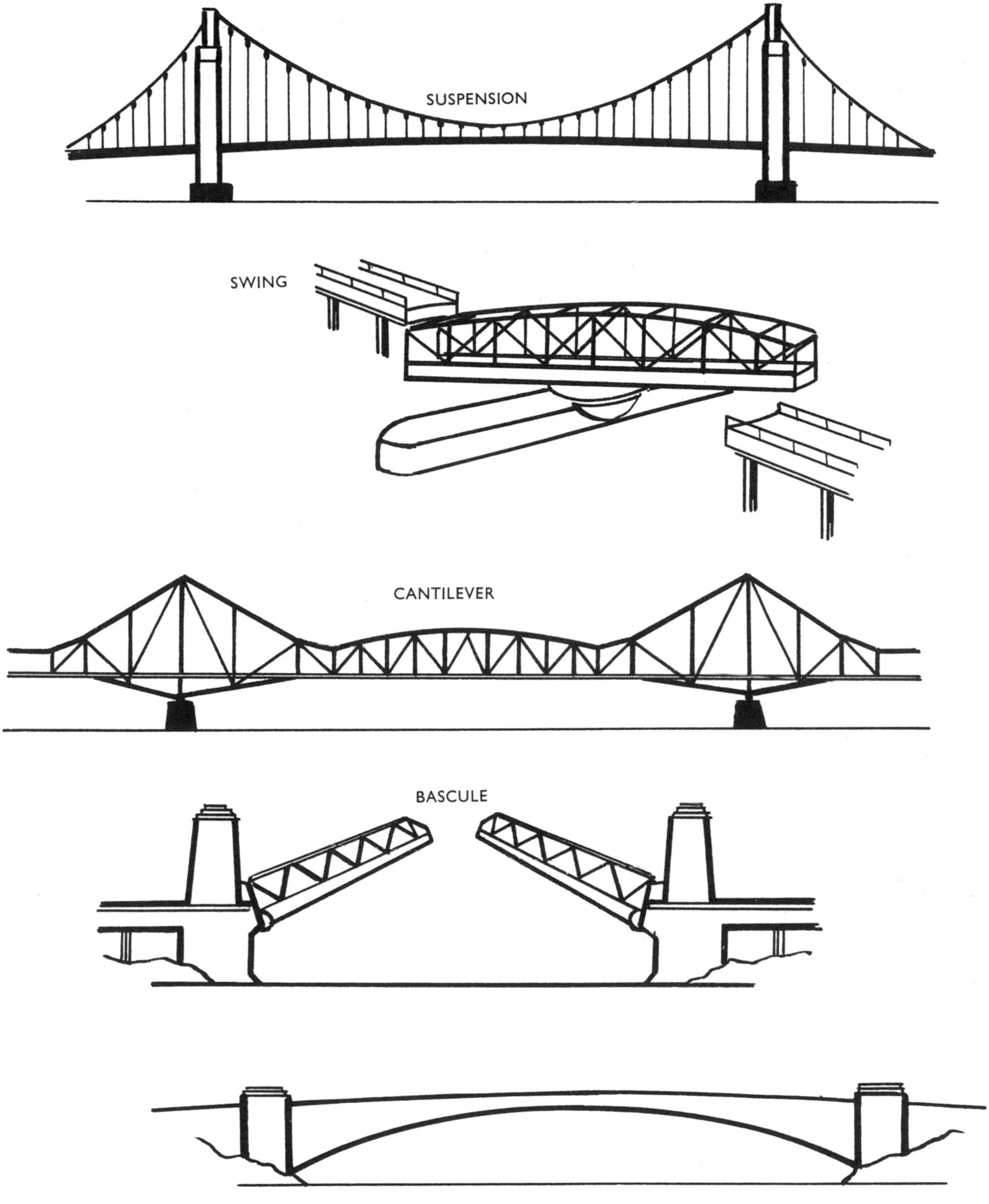

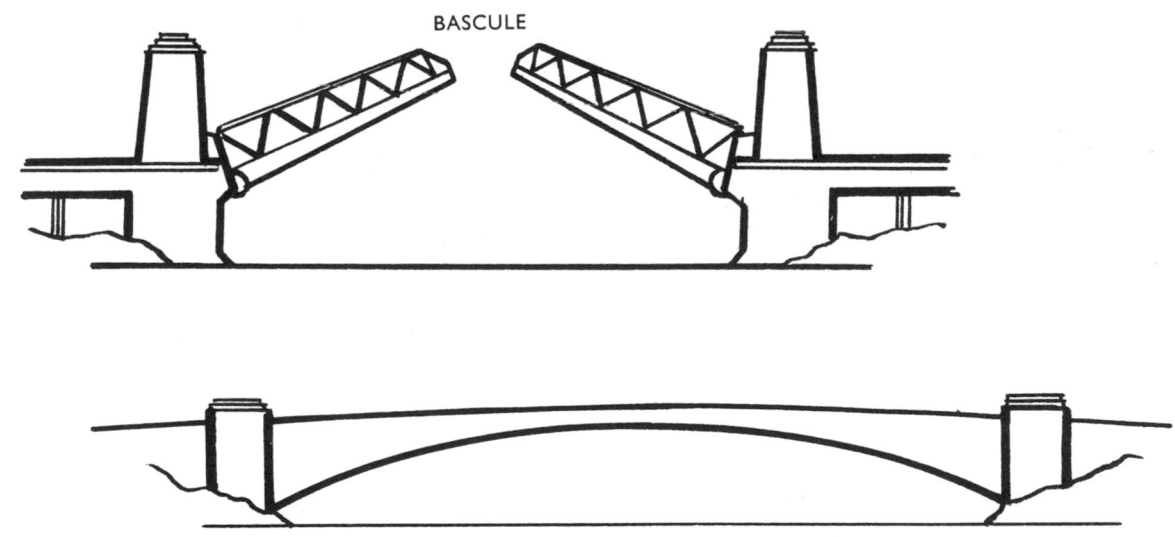

SUSPENSION

SWING

CANTILEVER

BASCULE

MODERN REINFORCED CONCRETE BRIDGE

53

streets too expensive for anything but a short stay, there still remain too many cars. Priced out of parking in the centre, they gather on the fringe of the parking meter zone and transfer the problem of congestion to the new areas. The volume of car traffic must be reduced if cities are to survive. A ban could be placed on all but essential cars entering the central zone and all other passengers would have to use public transport. This means that public transport must be good, reasonably priced and plentiful. Driving in city centres could be made expensive by some form of locked meter on all cars. It would be started by impulses from equipment buried in the road as a car entered the central zone, and stopped again as it left. The meters would be read periodically at official stations and a bill for using the central area sent to the car owner.

Another way is to reduce the size of

An experimental gas turbine truck developed by the Ford Motor Co. of America. Designed for long hauls across the States of America it has a refrigerator, cooker, sink and toilet for the driver.

These two pictures show the "Scamp" electric car made by Scottish Aviation. The Electricity Council who are leading the development in Britain will probably base their model on the Scamp. It will be capable of speeds up to 40 m.p.h.

DAG 908C

The Tokyo/Haneda monorail crosses a three-level highway.

cars. A very interesting design for a town saloon seating three has recently been put forward. The car is wide, seating three side by side, but is short enough to be parked end on to the kerb, so that three can park in the space normally occupied by one car and its "manœuvring room".

There is little doubt that experts like Professor Colin Buchanan were right in declaring that public transport would have to cater more for peak-hour traffic and that some form of subsidy for public transport is inevitable. Many European cities already subsidise their public transport and in the United States, public transport is now being actively encouraged by the Government.

Public transport in cities is best provided by underground railways, which have their own tracks and take up no surface area. Part of the new Bay Area Rapid Transit System—a high-speed railroad being built to serve San Francisco and neighbouring cities and towns —will run underground.

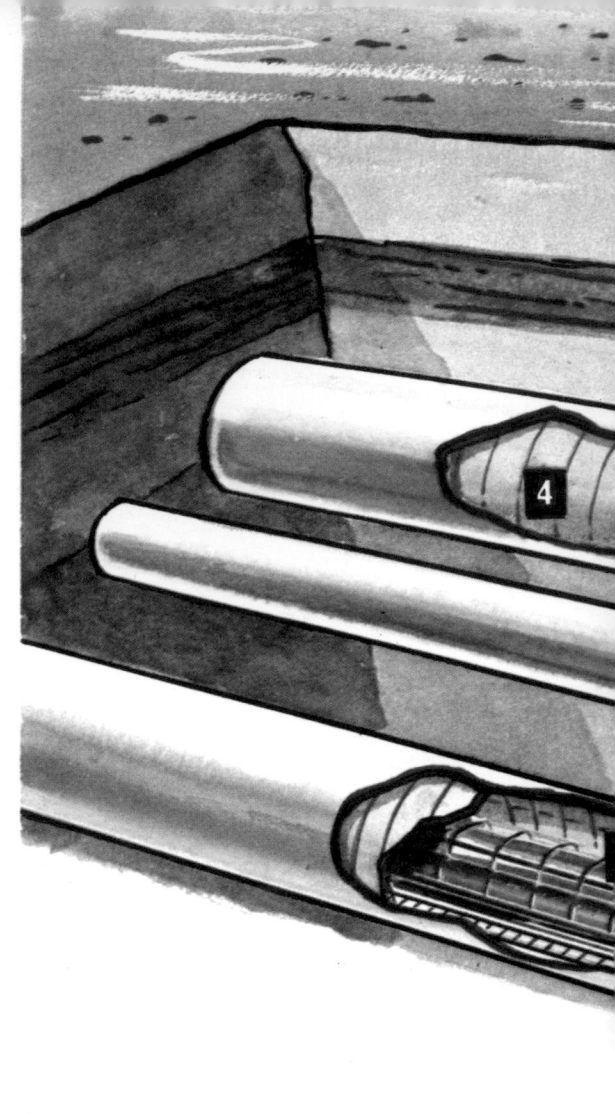

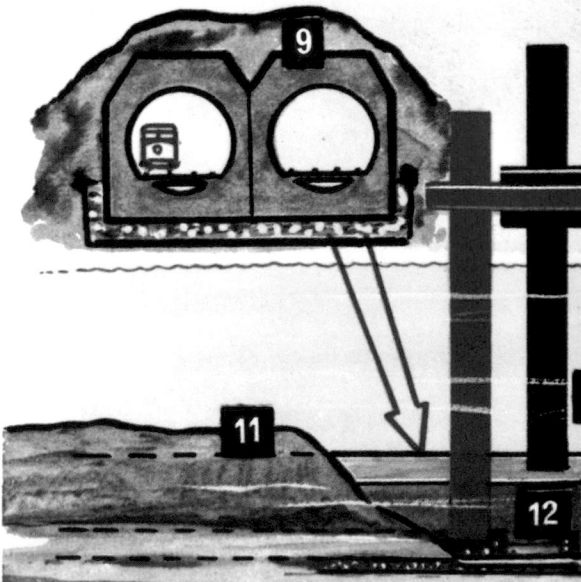

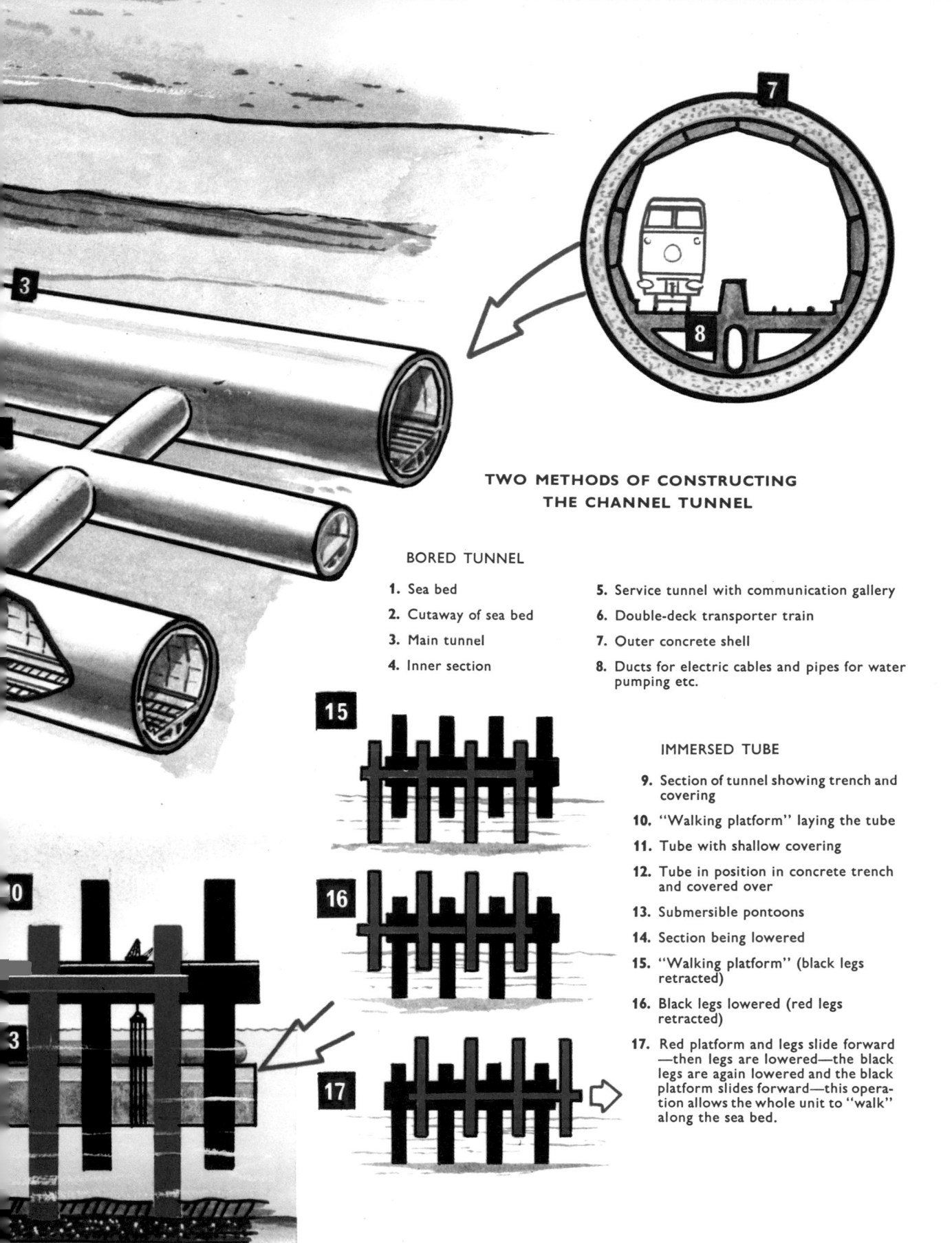

Above: The 13,821 ton passenger/cargo liner *Chitral* of P. & O. Orient Lines engaged in Far Eastern Mail Service.

Below: General cargo coaster of Tyne–Tees Shipping Co. Ltd.

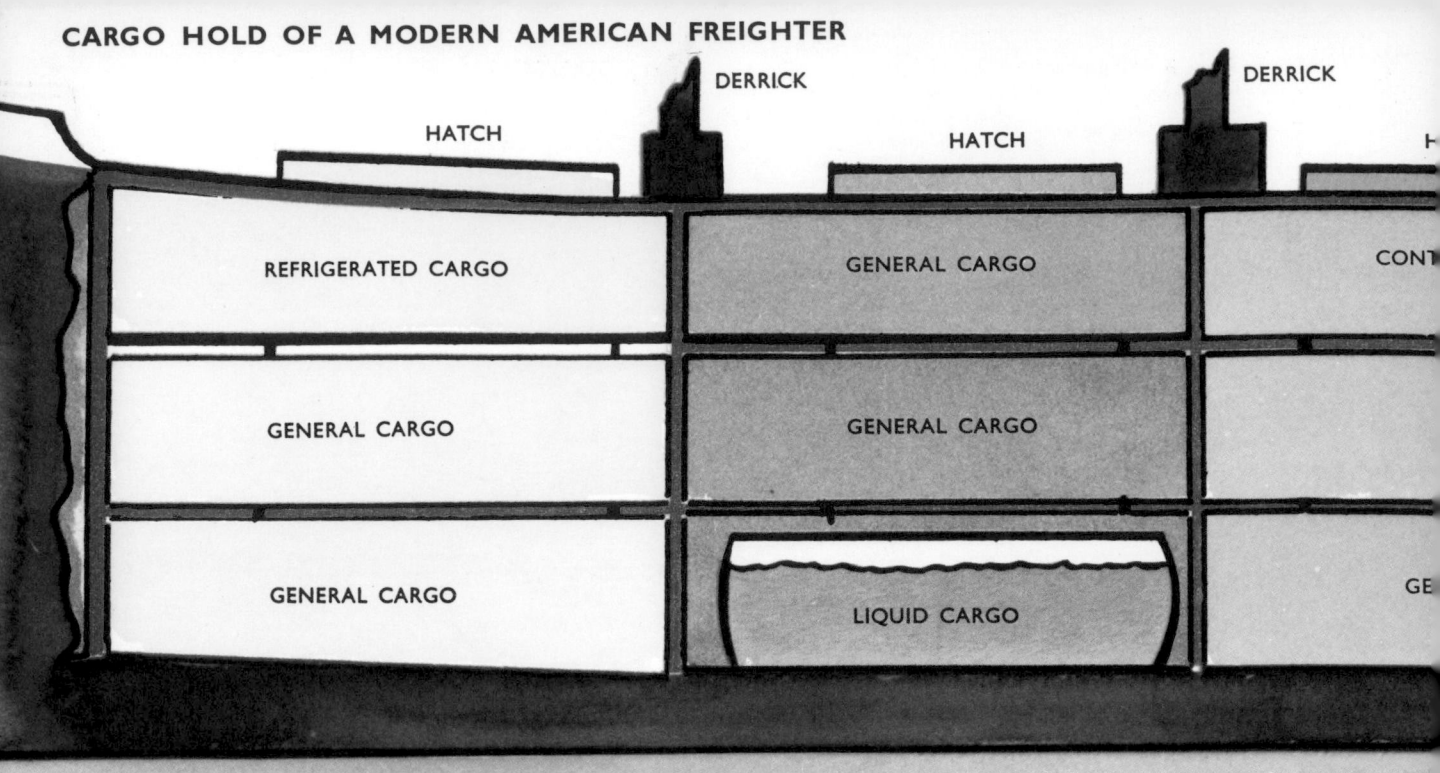

DERRICK

DERRICK

HATCH

HATCH

REFRIGERATED CARGO

GENERAL CARGO

CONT

GENERAL CARGO

GENERAL CARGO

GENERAL CARGO

LIQUID CARGO

GE

a broker operating on one of the world's shipping exchanges. The oldest and best known of these is the Baltic Exchange in London. The Exchange first began when the captains of ships engaged in the Baltic Sea trade met merchants in a London coffee house in order to do business. Since those early days the Baltic Exchange has grown enormously and its activities cover the whole world. The larger part of the world's tramp shipping business, in fact, is carried out through the Exchange.

The tramp ship is usually hired for a single voyage, or perhaps a series of consecutive voyages. On the other hand it might be hired on "time charter", that is to say for a certain period of time, during which the person who charters the vessel can use it in any trade he chooses, subject to agreed exceptions. Liner companies may charter tramp ships from time to time. There is a growing tendency for

tramp ships to be hired out on a contract basis in certain trades for a good number of years ahead. This applies particularly to more specialised ships such as tankers and ore carriers.

Industrial Carriers

Ships like oil tankers and ore carriers make up a special branch of the shipping industry known as industrial carriers. Oil tankers and ore carriers are designed for work with particular industries. The oil companies, for instance, have large fleets of their own tankers, but they also rely on chartering tramp tankers. Much the same applies to the steel companies, particularly in the United States and several European countries. British and Japanese steel companies rely to a much larger extent on chartering ore carriers. The aluminium companies too have large fleets of their own bauxite or

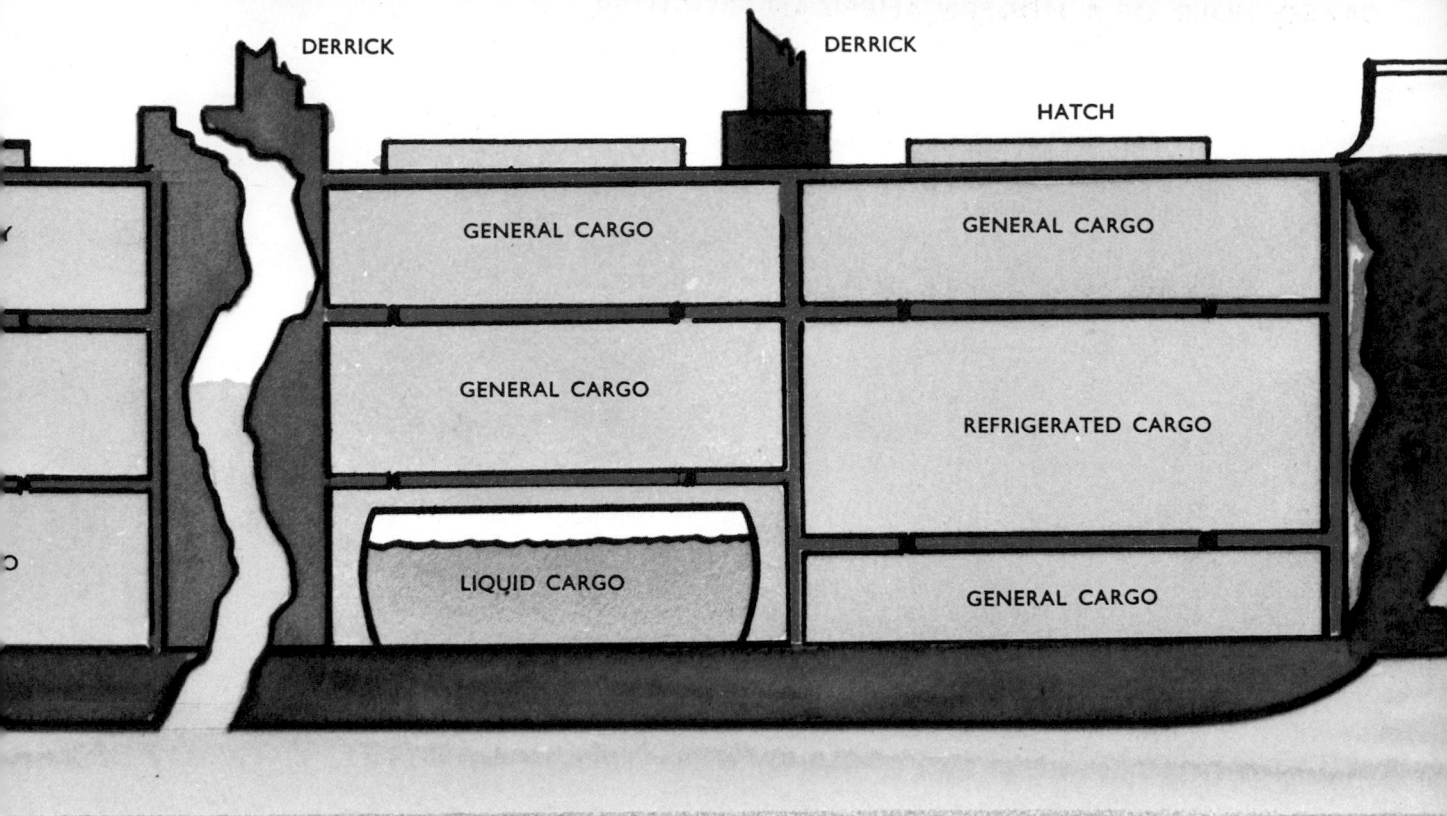

The hold arrangement of a typical modern cargo liner. The ship is designed to carry a variety of cargo, liquid, refrigerated container. The positioning of derricks near the hatches ensures fast and efficient cargo handling.

aluminium ore carriers, and they too rely to some extent on chartering. Newsprint and bulk sugar vessels are other important types of industrial carrier.

Iron ore, for example, is a very heavy cargo and a special design of hull is necessary to carry it if the most economic transport service is to be provided. Ore is loaded by special shore machinery in most ports and unloaded by grabs. Because of this, hopper-type holds with large hatch openings are provided in ore carriers, but it is not necessary to fit derricks for handling the cargo.

Millions of tons of iron ore are transported by sea every year, in addition to other ores such as bauxite and manganese. The trend is towards bigger and bigger carriers, since the larger the ship the cheaper the cost of transport per ton.

Tankers

Most tankers are used to carry petroleum products in bulk. They transport crude oil from the oil fields of the Middle East, the Caribbean and the Gulf of Mexico to the refineries, where the crude oil is processed to make paraffin, aviation fuel, automobile fuel and so on. Tankers are also used to transport these refined products from the refineries.

75

It is easy to recognise a tanker. The engine-room is always placed aft near the stern. The same applies to the crew's quarters. Tankers usually have the navigating bridge and superstructure just forward of amidships (or the middle of the ship). On the most modern tankers the midships superstructure is done away with and the bridge and superstructure placed aft near the stern. The tanker, of course, needs nothing in the way of derricks or cranes—except small ones for handling stores and engine-room equipment—since the cargo is loaded or unloaded entirely by pumps and hoses, or pipelines.

When fully loaded, tankers lie very low in the water, and this is another feature that makes them easy to recognise. However there is no danger of flooding from the waves which may pour over the decks in rough weather since the hatches are very small and the cargo tanks themselves have compartments like a honeycomb. Tankers usually have a raised catwalk running fore and aft which enables the crew to pass safely along the length of the vessel in stormy seas. In some of the more modern tankers—and in ore carriers too—underdeck wing passages are provided for this purpose instead of open catwalks.

Special Ships

There are a great number of vessels of different kinds which provide services to shipping, but which are not, strictly speaking, proper forms of transport. Important examples of these are cable laying and cable repair ships, ice breakers, weather ships, oil rigs and their service craft, dredgers and light vessels.

76

SECTIONISED CARGO SHIP

THE SHIP CARRIES A SPECIALLY DESIGNED FLOATING COMPARTMENT CAPABLE OF FLOATING FREELY WHEN THE PARENT SHIP HAS FLOODED HER BALLAST TANKS AND UNLOCKED THE CONTAINER. IT (THE PARENT) IS THEN READY TO PICK UP ANOTHER CONTAINER

How Ships are Operated

A great deal of complicated work is necessary before merchant ships—and this includes passenger liners—can be got ready to make their voyages. A liner's sailing schedules, for example, must be carefully worked out in advance. These schedules must be widely advertised so that people can know when the ships are sailing and where they are sailing to. The big passenger companies have their offices in the big cities, and these offices, as well as travel agencies, will do their best to fill the ship for every voyage.

The job of seeing passengers on board the ship on the day of sailing—passing them through the customs and immigration and getting their baggage on board—is fairly simple compared with the work that has to be done to ensure their comfort during the voyage. This work starts

AST TANKS

CARGO CONTAINER

as soon as the previous passengers have left the ship. In the case of one of the big Atlantic liners it has to be carried out within a turn-round period of 48 hours, or less, every week during the busy times of the year.

The first thing is to remove all signs of the previous passengers of the ship. While departing passengers are perhaps still going through the Customs, vacuum cleaners and floor polishers, mops, brooms and squeegees will be busily at work cleaning decks, alleyways, cabin floors and public rooms. At the same time carpenters, joiners and painters will be repairing any damage. The library, the cinema and the shops and showcases will have to be restocked.

Machinery throughout the ship, as well as navigating equipment and safety and firefighting gear, is overhauled. All this maintenance and cleaning is, of course, a continuous process carried out at sea as well as in port, but some of the work can only be done when the ship is in port.

Meanwhile stocks of every kind must be replaced. The *Queen Elizabeth*, for example, takes on some 5,000 tons of fresh water and 8,000 tons of oil fuel for every voyage. For a complement of over 2,000 passengers and 1,000 crew the ship's catering needs are measured in tons. A normal loading of provisions might include 20 tons of meat, 10 tons of fresh fish, 45 tons of vegetables and about 5 tons of fruit.

The amount of provisions required depends, of course, not only on the number of passengers and crew, but also on the length of the voyage.

Nowadays, since the coming of refrigeration, it is no longer necessary to carry live sheep, cows and hens in order to

77

supply fresh meat during long voyages at sea. Nor does a ship's company have to live on a diet of salt pork and hard tack, washed down with brackish water. Larger ships carry machinery which can distill hundreds of tons of fresh water from sea water daily.

With refrigeration and new methods of deep freezing the problems of a liner's catering department are made simpler. Fresh vegetables can be served up in any climate, and fresh milk can be frozen into solid blocks for use later.

Many changes have also occurred in the ship's galley. Dish washing machines, glass washing machines, electric mixers and infra-red grills make catering easier than it was in the past.

A revolution has changed the face of sea travel in recent years, and it is now safer and more comfortable than ever before.

Cargo Handling

The wide variety of goods carried by a modern cargo liner calls for an organisation which can cope with an amazing amount of complicated work. At one time or another the liner's cargo can be made up of such widely different things as textiles, radio equipment, whisky, foodstuffs of all kinds, tea, coffee, chemicals, machinery and even wild animals for zoos. Most of these items come in many different forms of packing—bags, bales, boxes, crates, drums and casks for example.

The collecting and organisation of the liner's cargo is mainly the responsibility of the liner company's outward freight department. The larger exporting companies generally have their own shipping departments which are in regular contact with the outward freight department, but smaller exporters will use the services of forwarding agents. A great amount of paper work is naturally involved. Every consignment must be properly marked and a bill of lading made out for it. The bill of lading is more than a ticket for the voyage; it is also a receipt and a contract of carriage, and a copy must be shown by the consignee (the person for whom the goods are intended) to prove identity and authority to receive the goods. In addition Customs clearance must be obtained, and sometimes import or export licences, or, again, consular certificates. A cargo manifest must also be prepared: this gives details of every item of cargo the ship carries. All these documents must be made out before the ship sails.

Every item of cargo should arrive alongside the ship for loading, but sometimes items which have been booked fail to appear and unexpected goods may arrive in the hope of finding space available. The shipowner has little or no control over the times at which, or the order in which, goods will arrive for loading. This makes the loading of a cargo difficult, because there are so many things that have to be taken into account. Heavy goods, of course, cannot be stowed on top of more fragile ones. Cartons of soap or crates of oranges cannot be stowed next to chests of tea owing to the risk of contamination. Care must be taken that bags of sugar are not likely to be spoiled by condensation from the ship's side. Finally, special precautions have to be observed when loading and carrying of explosives and inflammable materials.

To make matters more difficult cargo

Right: The 70-ton boom of a freighter of United States Lines lifts a container and (below) places it in one of the holds.

is often taken on at a whole number of loading ports, for unloading at a range of ports on the other side of the world. Thus goods loaded at the first port may be wanted at the first unloading port. It is vital that they should not be buried under a pile of other goods destined for later ports. The stability of the ship, too, is of very great importance. Care must be taken to see that the weights are properly placed throughout the holds. The question of stability is particularly important when heavy items are involved, or when cargo has to be carried on deck. There have often been cases where cargo has shifted during storms and has placed the ship in great danger.

Stowage problems are not so complicated, of course, when it comes to dry-cargo tramps and industrial carriers, which usually are dealing with large quantities of a single item. Even so, stability is still important and special care must be taken over the distribution of water ballast if the ship is only partly loaded. (Ballast is heavy material such as gravel, sand, or metal, but usually water in the case of modern ships, placed in an empty or nearly empty ship to keep it steady and stable.) Precautions have to be taken too when a ship is carrying grain in bulk since this behaves like a semi-liquid. Without special attention a grain cargo will tend to flow from side to side with the rolling of the ship, just as any normal liquid would do. When carrying grain the large holds of a tramp ship have to be divided up into smaller spaces by means of temporary bulkheads of timber—or sometimes steel or aluminium—often the top of the cargo is covered with grain in bags to prevent the

cargo "flowing".

Liquid cargoes are the simplest to handle, although special care must be taken if they are inflammable like oil. After every cargo is unloaded, the tanks must be freed of gases to avoid the danger of explosion.

Whether a ship is a liner, a tramp, a tanker or an industrial carrier her machinery and equipment as well as her hull must be carefully looked after. Every year a ship has to be put into dry dock so that the underwater parts can be inspected. Every four years she must undergo a survey by one of the classification societies such as American Bureau of Shipping, or Lloyd's Register of Shipping whose officials are responsible for specifying such repairs and replacements as they think necessary. These repairs and replacements may cover the main and auxiliary machinery, deck machinery (such as cranes and winches) electrical gear, navigational, life-saving and fire protection equipment or even the hull itself.

Above: the Shell tanker *Oscilla*

Centre: The tanker *Orissa* of Trident Tanker Lines

Left: Cargo ship *Patonga* of P. & O. Orient Lines

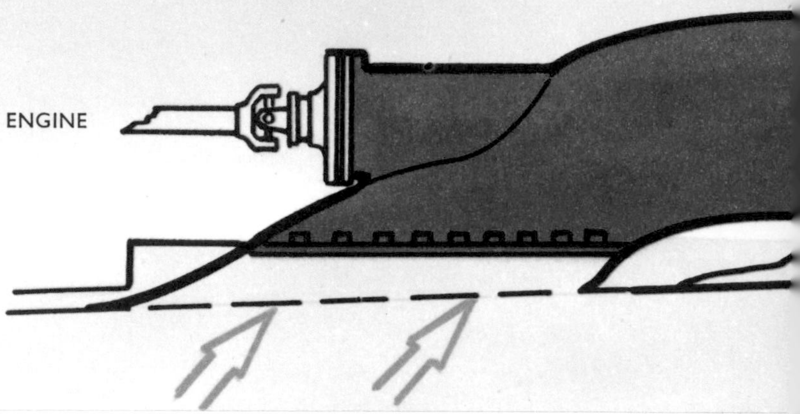

SHAFT TO ENGINE

NUCLEAR CARGO SUBMARINE

For many years ideas have been put forward for cargo-carrying
submarines. Here is one atomic project; a giant submarine
propelled by nuclear reactor and steam turbines. Such a craft, it
is believed, could carry large quantities of cargo at high speed
deep under the surface of the sea. The picture clearly shows the
huge cargo holds in the forepart of the vessel.

1. The hatch

2. Main controls

3. Ballast Tanks

4. Control and living quarters in "blister"

5. Reactor

6. Turbines

7. Propulsion motors

82

THE DOWTY TURBOCRAFT

Water is taken in through a grating (indicated by arrows) in the bottom of the hull, then through a two stage compressor—this increases the pressure. The water is then forced out of the nozzle at the back—so driving the boat forward.

Harbours and Ports

In its simplest form a harbour is a refuge for ships. It is a sheltered arm of the sea in which vessels can find protection from storms, where they might be built and launched and taken for repair. There are usually also means of loading and unloading cargoes from ships.

There are two main sorts of harbours —natural and artificial. Natural harbours are generally found in the mouths of rivers or in enclosed bays on the sea-coast. The land surrounding them gives protection from bad weather, and a true natural harbour needs no breakwater or piers to give that protection. Some of the world's most famous natural harbours can be seen at Sydney, San Francisco, New York (where the harbour is set in a river) and Trincomalee in Ceylon.

Artificial harbours, on the other hand, need breakwaters and piers to shelter ships from the effects of the weather. Madras harbour in India and Dover harbour are good examples. Some harbours, for example, combine both natural and artificial features.

No one knows when the first artificial harbours were built, although natural harbours set in bays or in the mouths of rivers have been used from the earliest times. There is evidence of a sea trade between Egypt and Crete more than 6,000 years ago, and naturally harbours must have been found for the ships.

It was not until the beginning of the nineteenth century that harbour building began to follow the tremendous development in sea transport. About that time it was possible to see many of the shapes and features of the seaports of modern times.

84

An aerial photograph of Dover harbour.

Lighthouses are signposts of the sea. Some of them, like the one shown in the picture, mark dangerous rocks. The foghorn (1) gives distinctive blasts when visibility is poor. The lantern house (2) encloses the powerful lenses and lamp mechanism (3). Repairs can be carried out to the equipment in the workshop (4 and 5). Sleeping quarters for the lighthouse crew are provided (6) and below them is the living room (7).

The loading room (8) is equipped with a crane to take on supplies. Food and general stores are kept in a special room (9), whilst oil fuel for the lamp is stored on the floor below (10). Access to the lighthouse is through the main entrance (11). Fresh water supplies are kept in tanks (12).

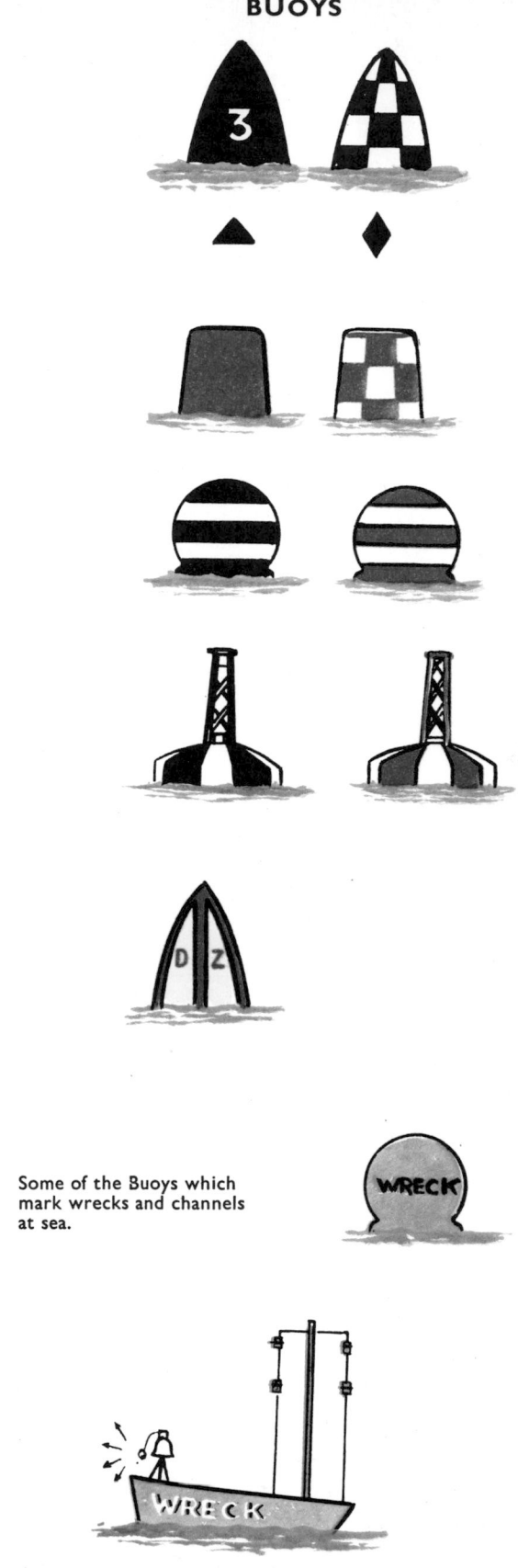

The harbours of today with their breakwaters, piers, jetties and docks are very complicated. An amazing amount of engineering work goes into making them good shelters for ships and at the same time to provide all the facilities needed so they can handle millions of tons of cargo. Cranes, storage sheds and oil tanks have to be built and railways have to be either laid down or improved so that goods can be carried to and from the harbour. In many cases there are special docks or slipways where ships can be repaired.

Most of the great harbours and ports of the world are part of or close to cities, but there are ports situated in remote places of the world where the inhabitants are few and far between. In northern Sweden, Labrador, Liberia and certain places in Brazil and Chile are seaports which handle large amounts of iron ore. Many of these ports exist solely to provide a place where the ore can be taken for loading on ships. The equipment of these ports is very special: mechanical loading devices which can fill ship's holds at the rate of many thousands of tons a day. The ore is carried by ship to the big industrial countries of the world like the United States, Britain, Japan, Germany and France. At these places the cargoes are unloaded by grabs at special terminals which are conveniently placed for the steelworks. Such iron ore terminals may just form one part of a seaport's activities.

Grain is another important cargo, and there are ports in the world which exist mainly to handle these cargoes. The main grain loading ports are in British Columbia, the Great Lakes of America, the

Some of the Buoys which mark wrecks and channels at sea.

Gulf of Mexico and various parts of Australia. In these places, large numbers of ships are loaded by means of grain elevators. At the journey's end the cargoes are sucked out of the holds of the ships pneumatically through pipes and go directly into grain mills alongside the dock or are put into barges to be taken to mills farther inland.

Unlike the iron ore ports, the grain ports usually handle other types of cargo as well. Thus timber is shipped from British Columbia, cotton from the Gulf of Mexico and dairy produce from Australia.

There is no such thing as a typical port. All ports are different. Some like the ore loading ports of Sweden have a very different job to do than ports like Southampton or New York. Yet Southampton and New York, although both of them handle passengers, are very different from each other in shape and layout. The same is true of other great ports of the world. Some of these ports are located on rivers. Where the river is large and deep enough as is the case with the Mississippi, the Ganges, the Rhine or the River Plate, the important ports can be located a good distance upstream. In some places, where the rise and fall of the tide presents no great problems, as in New York or Rotterdam, it is only necessary to provide quays for the ships to come alongside. In other ports, such as London and Liverpool, the rise and fall of the tides makes it essential to build enclosed docks, with entrance locks that are opened at high-tide to let in ships, but closed at other times to keep sufficient depth of water in the dock. Sometimes, when there are no river entrances the entire harbour, like the one at Genoa in Italy, is artificially built out into the sea.

The most important ports have to handle almost every kind of cargo. The ports of Europe and North America, in particular, are equipped with large numbers of dockside cranes, although in many other parts of the world liners and other ships have to rely on their own derricks and cranes for loading and unloading cargoes. Dockside sheds and warehouses are provided for receiving, sorting and dispatching cargoes. There are refrigerated cold stores for perishable goods like fruit, meat and dairy products; silos for storing grain and sugar; facilities for handling passengers and their baggage. Oil storage tanks, because of the risk of fire, are usually placed some distance away from other port activities.

A great deal of general cargo traffic today is handled in containers. This is especially true of the short sea routes, like those between Britain and Europe. The containers can be transferred directly from the holds of the ships to trucks or railroad wagons, or vice versa. Many ports are also equipped to deal with what is called "roll-on roll-off" transport. Here road and rail vehicles are shipped complete with their loads. The road or rail truck containing the goods makes the voyage on a specially built ship which will probably resemble a car or train ferry. The vehicle will leave the ship at its port of call and then go on to its final destination. This method of sending goods saves considerable time, trouble and money.

As we have seen, other kinds of facilities are needed to serve the ships that use a port. Docks and repair yards have to be

THE HARWICH TRAIN FERRY

Above: Swiss Interfrigo wagons being loaded on to the *Suffolk Ferry*.

Right: The *Essex Ferry* leaving the Harwich Terminal for the Continent.

provided together with oil tanks for refuelling. There are tugs to handle ships —particularly large ships—entering or leaving the port. Firefighting and salvage vessels must be kept ready in case of accident. Dredgers, too, are often needed to keep the entrances, channels and berths of the harbour from silting up with mud.

Canals and Inland Waterways

Canals and inland waterways are very closely associated with sea transport. There are two types of canals: those which can be used by sea-going vessels and even large liners, and barge canals which are usually smaller. As a rule barge canals are a form of inland transport and need not be connected with the sea at all.

Canals have a long and interesting history. About 500 B.C. one of the Egyptian pharoahs started building a canal be-

tween the Nile and Red Sea—surely a forerunner of the modern Suez Canal. Three centuries later it is believed that a canal was built in China. The Romans were very interested in canals. But the first great canal—the Grand Canal of China connecting three rivers—was opened during the thirteenth century. In Europe, Emperor Charlemagne planned a system of canals to link the rivers Main, Rhine and Danube.

Before the coming of the railways and in the days when roads were bad, the canal proved to be the best way of moving people and goods, and although canals as such are artificial waterways, rivers themselves naturally became part of a canal system.

The very early canals were built on one level, and of course, were only of use as a means of travelling through flat country. It was only with the invention of the lock that canals could be made to run "up and down hill". Locks are nothing more or less than a system of gates which allow ships to be raised or lowered between different water levels—a kind of liquid staircase, in fact. No one is certain where locks were first introduced; it may have been in either Holland or China during the fourteenth century. The French Canal du Midi, for example, which connects the Mediterranean with the Bay of Biscay, rises at one point to a height of 620 feet above sea-level.

Opposite: A typical harbour—the dotted lines indicate railway tracks from each berth.

The Great Lakes of North America form the most important system of inland water transport in the world. Below is the Iroquois Lock which leads into Lake Ontario.

Ship canals fall into two classes; those which connect two seas or lakes and those which provide access for ships to inland ports. The Panama Canal, for example, connects the Atlantic with the Pacific Ocean and the Manchester Ship Canal in England allows ships to sail inland to the city of Manchester.

The four most famous ship canals with a large international trade are the Suez, Panama, Manchester and Kiel. The Suez Canal crosses flat land and so needs no locks, while the Panama Canal passes through hilly country and has, of course, a system of locks. The Suez Canal was originally cut to shorten the sea voyage between Europe and India, which before it was built was only possible by sailing round the southern tip of Africa. Similarly the Panama Canal saves the long and possibly stormy trip round Cape Horn.

Since the Panama is not a sea-level canal the size of the ships passing through is limited by the size of the locks as well as by the width and depth. Much the same applies to the St. Lawrence Seaway, which enables ocean-going ships to reach the ports in the Great Lakes. The Great Lakes of North America form the most important system of inland water transport in the world. The five main lakes are Superior, Michigan, Huron, Erie and Ontario and some of the larger ones are almost miniature seas. Because the lakes are so near important centres of production—iron ore and coal-mines and wheat-fields—they are used to carry amazing amounts of goods. Every year something like 194,000,000 tons of goods are carried on them.

Most of the traffic of the Great Lakes is made up of heavy goods and special ships have been designed to carry these cargoes. The usual bulk freighter—except on Lake Ontario—is long and narrow and has the engine-room and crew quarters aft near the stern. These ships can pass from one lake to another by means of a system of canals.

Although the Great Lakes are well inland, three important waterways connect them with the sea—the St. Lawrence Seaway, which has already been mentioned, the New York canals, Hudson River—Lake Champlain, and the Lake Michigan to Mississippi waterway. All of these routes are fitted with locks.

Barge Canals

As mentioned earlier barge canals need not be connected with the sea, although some terminate in docks or harbours where ocean-going ships can lie. In Europe the chief canal networks can be found in France, Holland, Belgium, Germany, Sweden and Russia. In some cases the canal routes are linked up so that long through hauls are possible for international traffic. These canals are usually connected to large rivers such as the Rhine, the Danube, the Elbe and the Volga. Inland water transport was developed by making canals of difficult parts of their routes or by connecting rivers by specially built canals. The barges that travel on such canals and waterways need not be small; some of the German barges, for instance, are as big as 1,000 tons or more, with lengths of over 200 ft. and widths of up to 30 ft. On the other hand, where rivers and canals are not so wide, as in England, barges are much smaller.

Navigation and Safety

Despite the fact that modern science has produced many aids to navigation, seamen still depend on the magnetic compass and chart. But the magnetic compass which proved its usefulness over centuries has been replaced in many cases by the gyro-compass which is more dependable. The gyro-compass can be linked to an automatic pilot so that a ship's course is maintained without human aid. Even so, hand steering gear must always be provided in case of failure or breakdown.

In just a little over fifty years radio has become one of the most useful aids to the navigator. Not only can a radio direction-finder be used to find a ship's position from shore stations, but the vessel can be kept in touch with the latest reports from weather stations. Radio can, of course, receive or transmit distress signals—this was the earliest use of ships' radio.

Radar has helped to prevent many accidents and almost all ships are fitted with it. Radar can show on a screen the exact position of other ships. It will also mark the position of landmarks or buoys when they might otherwise be invisible because of darkness. For close navigation in narrow waters there are the Decca Navigator or Loran systems; these show the exact position of a ship on a chart to within a few feet. Another important piece of equipment is the echo-sounder which can give a continuous record of the depth of water underneath a ship's keel.

Lighthouses, Light Vessels and Buoys

In waters near the coast the navigator relies to a great extent on lighthouses, light vessels and buoys. Lighthouses are an old invention and date back many thousands of years. They are said to have been used in ancient Egypt, where priests apparently lit beacon fires. But the most famous lighthouse in history is the Pharos of Alexandria, regarded as one of the seven wonders of the world. It was built sometime between 283 and 247 B.C. and is said to have been some 600 ft. in height. The Romans built a number of lighthouses but although lighthouse building went on through the years it was not until the seventeenth and eighteenth centuries that many more towers were built. These contained either wood or coal fires to provide the warning light and were put up in many parts of Europe.

Lighthouses may be built on isolated rocks out at sea. They may be built on cliff tops, or on some other part of the shore. There are many different designs of lighthouse; some consist of a stone or concrete tower, others are of openwork steel construction and others, especially those which stand on a sandy sea-bed, are built on top of a caisson—a sort of hollow steel box which is subsequently filled with concrete. But whatever type a lighthouse may be, its purpose is to provide some sort of warning light. The earlier lighthouses were fitted with fixed lights which threw beams in all directions. But today most lighthouses are provided with apparatus to throw flashing beams of one form or another. The system of lenses used in modern lighthouses are complicated. In the past coal and wood fires, oil, coal gas and acetylene gas have been used to provide the light. More recently electric light has come into use. The older type of lighthouse had to be manned by a crew whose job it was to attend to the light and see it was replenished with fuel, but today more and more lighthouses are unmanned, and the lighthouse is only visited at regular intervals for maintenance.

As the name suggests light vessels are ships specially fitted with lamps. They might be called floating lighthouses. Light vessels are usually stationed in places where it would be difficult or impossible to build a lighthouse. They are moored to the sea-bed with special anchors.

Buoys are used throughout the world to mark the fringes of the channels which ships can safely use, to mark sunken wrecks or isolated rocks, and mark the position of telephone or telegraph cables. There are many different types in use. Some buoys are fitted with warning lights so that they are, in effect, miniature floating lighthouses. Others are provided with bells or whistles for warning purposes.

The nuclear cargo ship *Savannah* showing the nuclear reactor and propulsion system.

1. Reactor. **2.** Hot gas. **3.** Heat exchanger. **4.** Cool gas. **5.** Steam. **6.** Turbine. **7.** Drive shaft.

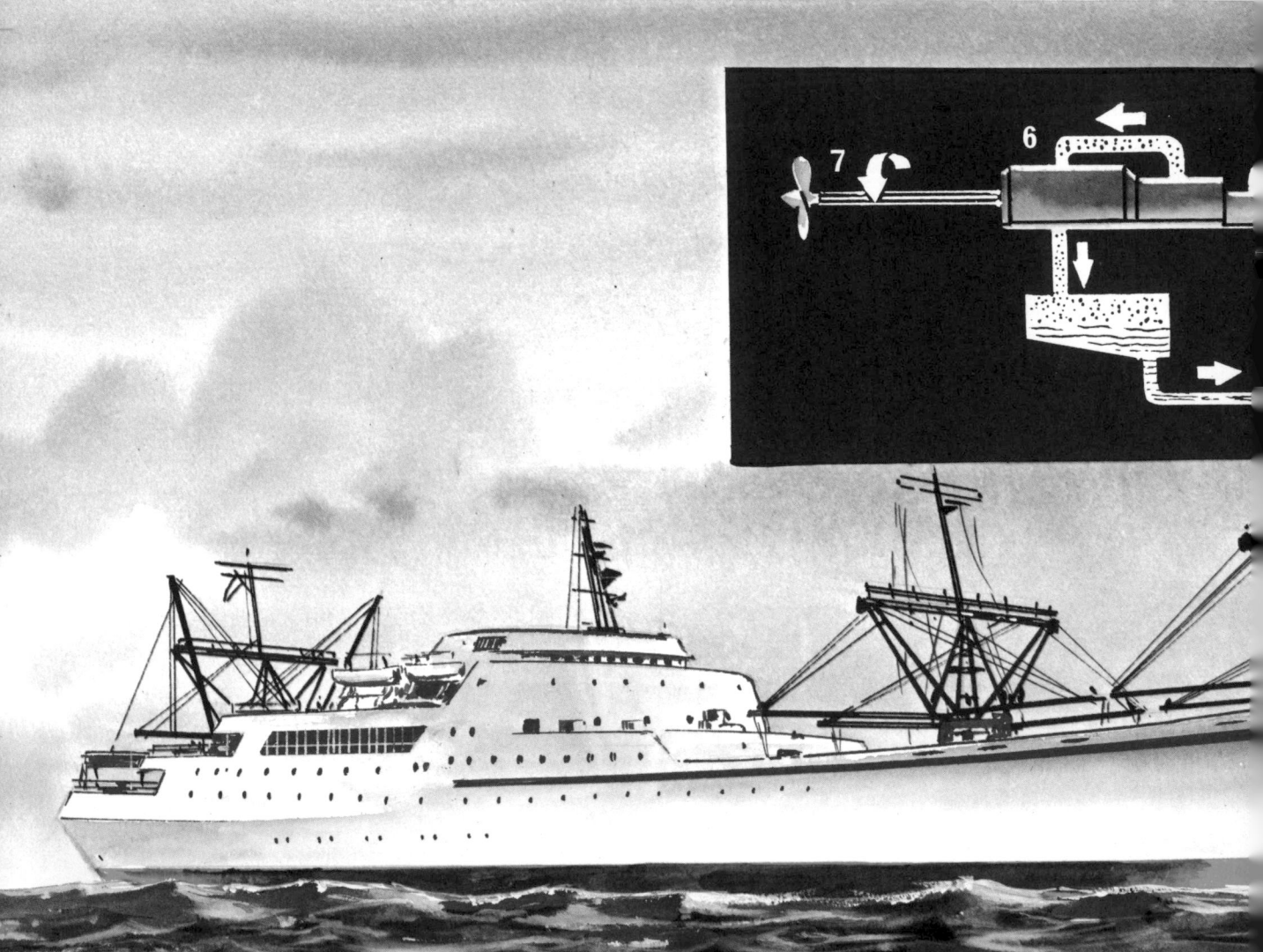

Lifeboats

The story of lifeboats is one of the most dramatic and exciting. It would be impossible to assess how many lives were lost in shipwrecks and accidents before lifeboat services were first established. Every year throughout the world lifeboats save many hundreds of lives.

An ordinary open boat is not suited to lifesaving in a stormy sea; the lifeboat has to be specially designed to carry out this work. The most important feature is that it should be unsinkable and as stable as possible. The forerunner of the lifeboat—although it was very different from more modern types—was built in the late eighteenth century by Lionel Lukin, an English coachbuilder. A few years later, Henry Greathead, another Englishman, designed a lifeboat which was given buoyancy by nearly 7 cwt. of cork. The boat, which lasted for over thirty years, saved hundreds of lives at sea. It was not long before people began to realise the importance of the lifeboat. Before the end of 1803 Greathead had built thirty-one boats—eighteen for England, five for Scotland and another eight for other countries.

By 1824 the Royal National Life-Boat Institution had been set up in Britain. The organisation helped to revolutionise the building of lifeboats and was a model for other lifeboat services all over the world. Some lifeboat services are run by the state, as in the case of the United States, where the service is carried on by the Coast Guard. In other countries it is voluntary, as in Britain. The United States Coast Guard also operates the international ice patrol which warns shipping of the position of icebergs in the North Atlantic sea lanes.

Safety at Sea

The heavy loss of life in 1912 when the passenger liner *Titanic* struck an iceberg on her first voyage gave rise to the series of international conventions on the safety of life at sea which now govern many of the safety measures which must be provided in ships. They specify, for example, the minimum number and types of lifeboat that must be carried in each kind of ship. In some cases inflatable life-rafts are now authorised, because of the difficulties sometimes experienced in launching the traditional type of lifeboat. The conventions also lay down minimum

SAVANNAH

95

Lifeboats

Above left: High speed air-sea rescue.

Above right: The "Anstruther Lifeboat".

Right: In-shore rescues can be carried out with this inflatable model.

standards of radio equipment and other life-saving equipment which must be carried. They also make regulations concerning the subdivision of the hull into watertight compartments, thus reducing the danger of sinking after a collision.

The international safety conventions also devote a great deal of attention to the prevention of fire, which is always a great danger at sea. Sprinkler systems are frequently installed, which automatically drench a compartment with water if the temperature rises to a dangerous level, but more attention has been paid in recent years to the introduction and use of fireproof materials, such as plastic substitutes for wooden bulkheads. When the liner *United States* was built it was claimed that the only objects in the ship which would burn were the pianos and the butchers' chopping blocks.

The danger of fire is obvious in oil

tankers, because of the inflammable nature of the cargo, and in ordinary dry-cargo ships too the danger exists, sometimes because of spontaneous combustion in the holds. Steam smothering lines are generally used to extinguish fires in holds, but some ships are equipped also with inert gas generators, which are used to prevent oxygen from feeding the flames. Foam extinguishers are provided to cope with engine-room fires.

Propelling Machinery

The invention of the steam engine started a revolution in merchant shipping. But the revolution did not take place suddenly. Many years passed by before steam finally replaced sail on the high seas. The early steam engines with their large cylinders were cumbersome affairs. They were also greedy for coal and it was difficult for early ships to carry a sufficient quantity. The first steamships all had paddle-wheels, and although the coming of the screw propeller helped to make ships more efficient, it was a long time before steamers were able to dispense with their sails.

A major advance came about with the invention of the steam turbine. Instead of cylinders the turbine has special rotors, driven by high-pressure super-heated steam, which are connected to the propellors through gears. Much more power can be developed by the turbine, and this is helped with the use of oil-fired instead of coal-fired boilers. In some cases turbines are used to drive electric generators which supply current to electric motors. The motors in turn drive the ship's propellers.

The next development in marine propulsion was the invention of the diesel

Two Early Steam Ships

Above: The *Chusan* built in 1852. She inaugurated the P & O mail service to Australia which took 80 days.

Left: The *William Fawcett* built in 1829 A Paddle Steamer which ran from Dublin to London till 1837 when she made regular trips to Spain.

97

THE HOVERCRAFT AND THE HYDROFOIL MAY HELP TO
REVOLUTIONISE TRANSPORT IN THE FUTURE. THE TOP PICTURE
SHOWS THE DESIGN FOR A LARGE SEA-GOING PASSENGER HOVER-
CRAFT. IN THE INSET (1) CAN BE SEEN THE BASIC PRINCIPLE OF
ALL HOVERCRAFT: A FAN DRAWS IN AIR, WHICH PASSES DOWN-
WARDS, SLIGHTLY COMPRESSED, TO PROVIDE A CUSHION OF AIR
UPON WHICH THE CRAFT RIDES SMOOTHLY. IN THE BOTTOM
PICTURE A HYDROFOIL TRAVELS AT SPEED. THE INSET (2) SHOWS
HOW THE FOILS FITTED ON THE BOTTOM OF THE HULL RAISE
THE HYDROFOIL HULL CLEAR OF THE WATER IN THE SAME WAY
THAT AN AIRCRAFT'S WINGS PROVIDE LIFT.

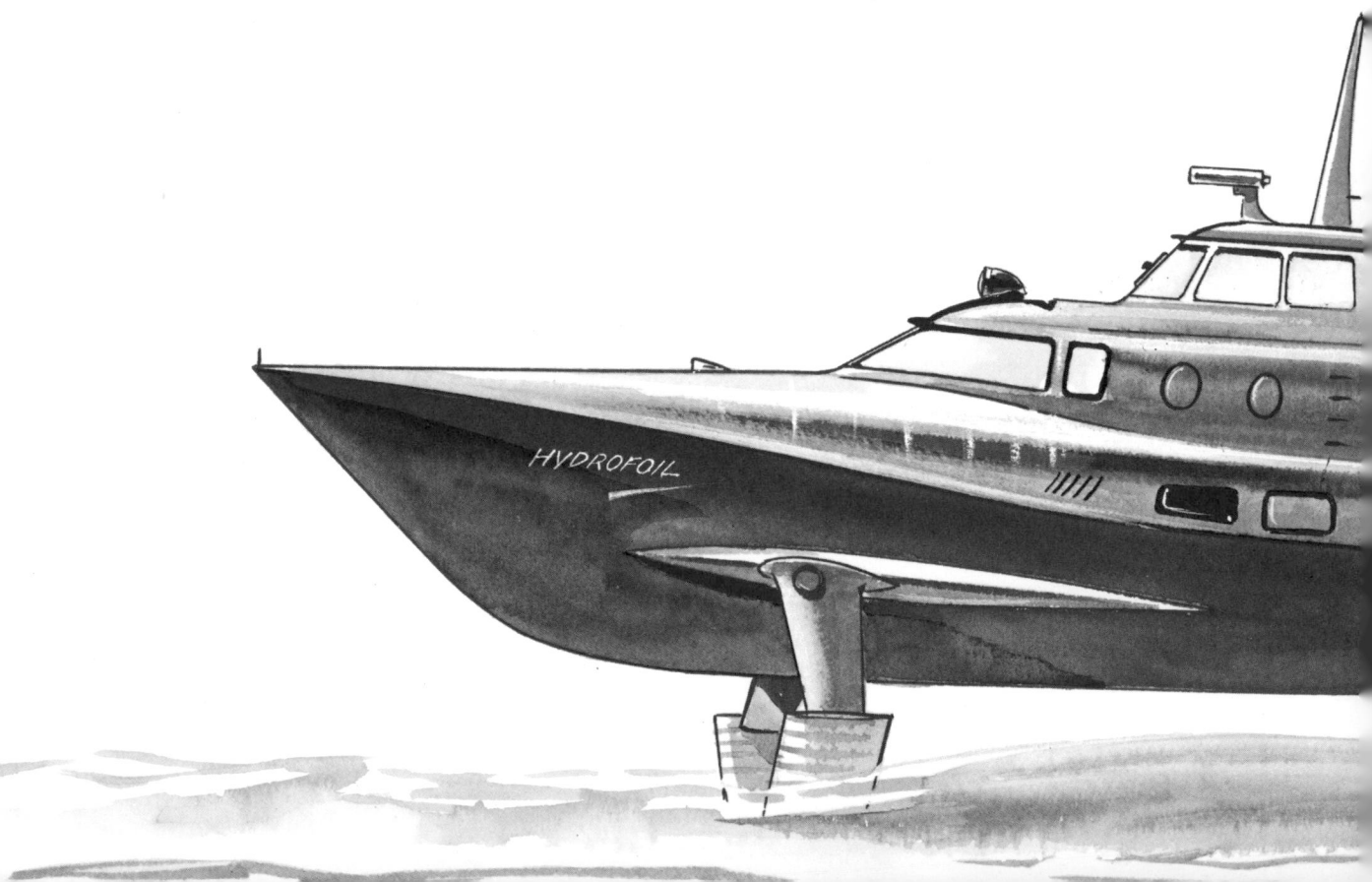

HYDROFOIL

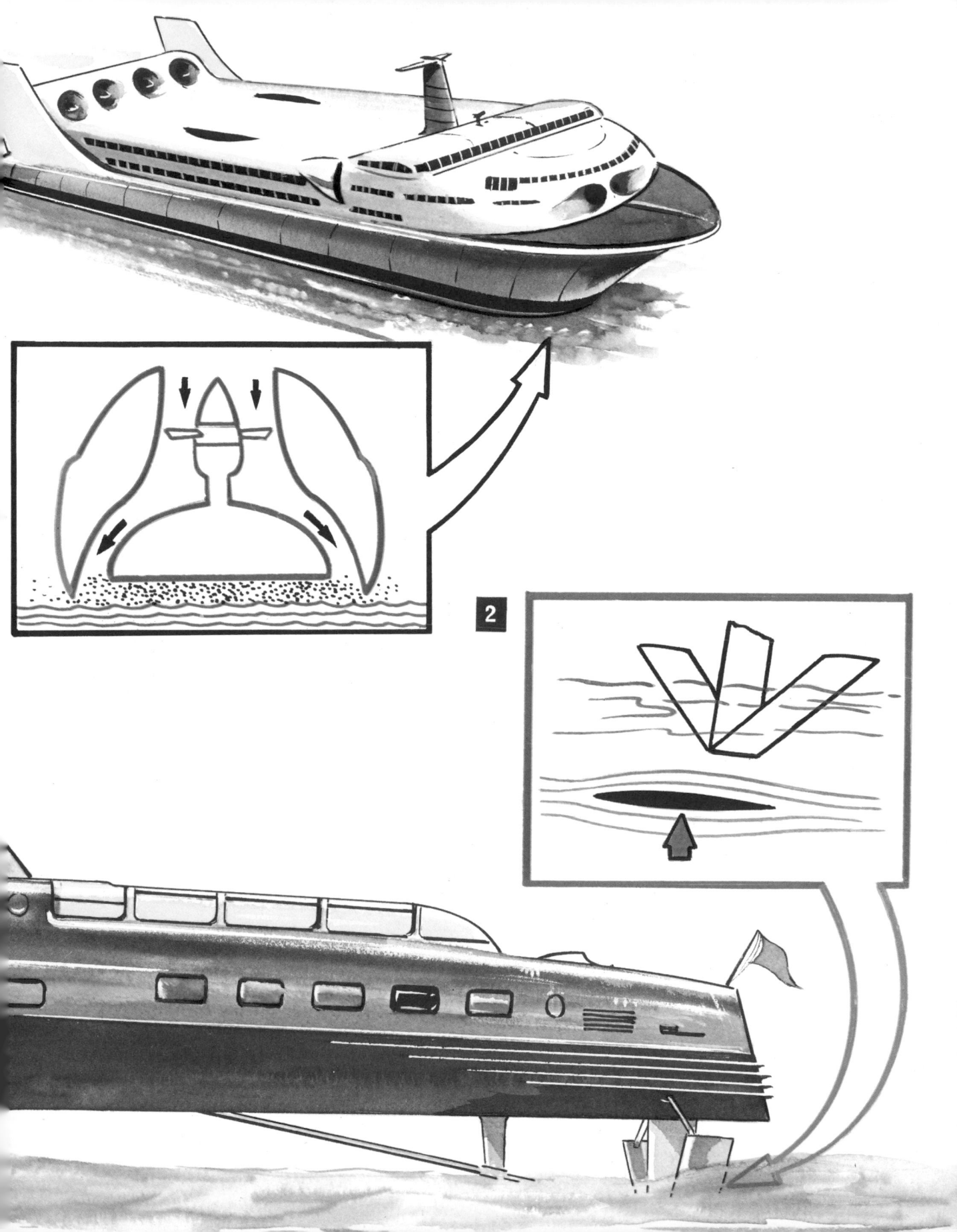

2

engine which has become increasingly popular.

There have been great hopes that nuclear power could be used for propelling a ship. But it is a costly process. The nuclear reactor is merely a substitute for burning ordinary fuel to produce steam for driving turbines. A nuclear reactor cuts out the need for fuel tanks which always have to be refilled—the nuclear ship can go for years without having to refuel. This is the chief reason why nuclear reactors are so suitable for vessels like submarines and for the Russian ice breakers of the *Lenin* class, which have to operate long distances in places far away from fuel stores. But the weight of reactors and their shielding prevents a good deal of paying cargo being carried in a ship; and this is apart from the high cost of the reactor itself. The world's first nuclear passenger-cargo ship was the United States' *Savannah*.

Ships of the Future

Even if it takes many years before nuclear propulsion for ships becomes a commercial proposition, great strides forward are still being made in marine

The twin propellers of the *Canberra* in dry dock at Southampton.

The bridge of the S.S. *France*.

engineering and shipbuilding and design. We are beginning to see the results in practice. To provide the power needed for the *Queen Mary* in 1934 two engine-rooms were required, each containing twelve boilers to supply steam to turbines driving four propellers. Six years later only twelve boilers in all were needed for the *Queen Elizabeth*. The new replacement for the *Queen Mary* will need only four boilers and two propellers to provide something like 110,000 shaft horsepower.

The saving in weight and space required from this more efficient machinery enables the same performance to be given by a much smaller ship. The new *Queen* will carry much the same number of passengers at much the same speed, but she will be of only about 58,000 tons gross, compared with more than 80,000 tons for the original *Queens*. She will need a much smaller engine-room. Furthermore, because of the use of aluminium alloys in her superstructure, her draught will be reduced to about 31 ft., some 10 ft. less than that of her predecessors, thus increasing the number of ports she can enter.

The automation of ships is becoming more commonplace every day. For years it has been possible for the navigating officer to control the engines of smaller ships directly from the bridge, instead of merely transmitting orders to the engine-room by telegraph. Cargo hatches can be opened and closed automatically by the touch of a button; and in some new tankers one man can control the complete unloading operations from a central control panel, from which he can tell how empty the tanks are.

Entirely new forms of marine transport are also well into practical stages of development. Hydrofoil craft, for example, have been used for a long time for short-stage sheltered-water passenger carrying, particularly in the Mediterranean, in Scandinavia and on the Swiss Lakes. When these craft reach a certain speed their hulls rise out of the water and they ride on a wing-shaped foil beneath the surface. This avoids the effects of wave resistance on the hull. So far these have been limited in size, but the United States Navy has built the prototype *Dennison*, of some 1,000 tons, on which further research is being carried out, and on some Russian rivers there are hydrofoil craft in service which can carry some 300 passengers at speeds believed to exceed 60 knots.

The hovercraft is being developed. Here the whole vessel is raised above the surface of the water on a cushion of air, and propelled forward by aircraft-type gas turbines. These vessels are freed

102

CAPTAIN COUSTEAU'S
STAR FISH UNDERWATER HOUSE

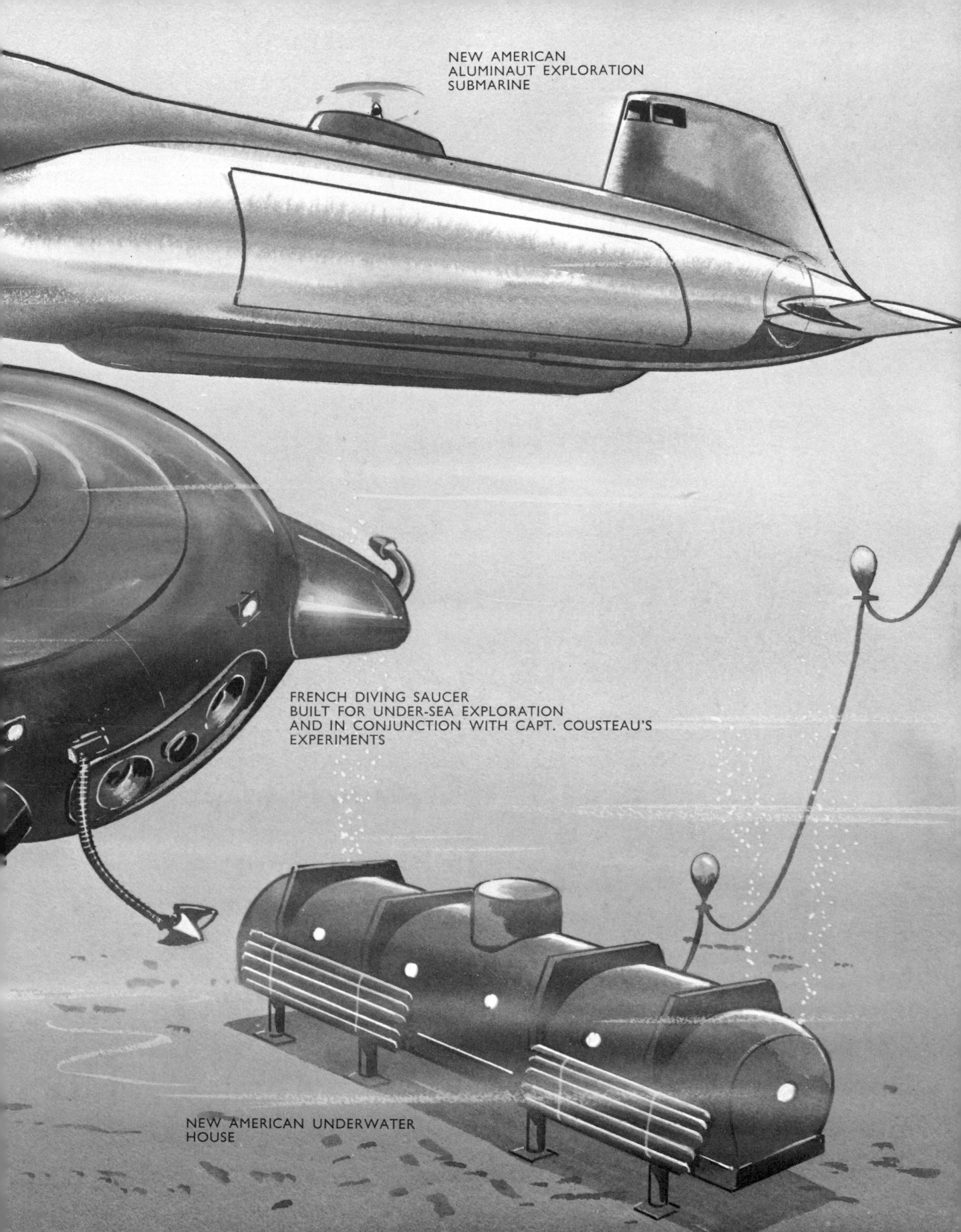

NEW AMERICAN
ALUMINAUT EXPLORATION
SUBMARINE

FRENCH DIVING SAUCER
BUILT FOR UNDER-SEA EXPLORATION
AND IN CONJUNCTION WITH CAPT. COUSTEAU'S
EXPERIMENTS

NEW AMERICAN UNDERWATER
HOUSE

The S.S. *France* leaving New York Harbour.

entirely from contact with the water. They can reach very high speeds in proportion to the power of their engines. Furthermore they can operate over flat land just as well so that they do not need elaborate port equipment—nothing more in fact than a shelving beach or a concrete slipway.

We are already seeing a great development of the "roll-on roll-off" principle, in which loaded vehicles are driven on and off over ramps at the bow or stern, or sometimes both. This is a further development of the "container ship" principle, in which goods are loaded in specially designed and sized containers for dis-charge on to land transport at the terminal. Both these principles we may see extended to all ocean routes for liner trades. Time spent in loading and discharging cargoes in port is the great enemy of the shipowner (and of the shipper and consignee) and much research and ingenuity is being spent on trying to reduce this costly item. Perhaps one day we will see ships designed on the railway locomotive principle, with propelling units detachable from the cargo-hull which can be left in port to discharge while the "engine" takes away another cargo unit which has previously been loaded.

AIR TRANSPORT

For thousands of years men have moved themselves and their goods by land and water. But travel by air is new; it is only a little over sixty years since the first controlled flight by a heavier-than-air machine was made by the Wright brothers. Let us see how flying has developed.

Although it was Orville Wright who made the first flight, the idea of flying goes back much further. According to the Greek legend Icarus flew too near the Sun, whose heat melted the wax by which his artificial wings were attached to his body. He was killed when he hit the ground and so became the first "casualty" in aviation history. In the fifteenth century Leonardo da Vinci, the great Italian painter and inventor, made many drawings of machines that he thought would fly, but none was actually built.

The first real step towards practical flight was made in 1783, when the first ascent was made by a hot-air balloon. This was designed by the French Montgolfier brothers, and two years later Blanchard and Jefferies crossed the English Channel in a balloon. The first flight of more than a thousand miles was made in 1859 in a balloon piloted by John Wise.

Thirteen years earlier, in 1846, John Stringfellow designed and built the first power-driven aeroplane model to fly.

In December, 1903, the Wright brothers' flight at Kitty Hawk, in the United States, took place and in July, 1909, Louis Bleriot made the first crossing of the English Channel by an aeroplane. In many ways 1909 was a vintage year for the early designers, for 100 miles was flown non-stop for the first time, and by the end of the year the speed and height records had been lifted to 47 m.p.h. and 1,426 ft. respectively. In 1914 the first scheduled airline began operations, between St. Petersburg and Tampa, Florida, a distance of 22 miles, using a Benoist flying-boat which carried two passengers.

During the First World War, between 1914 and 1918, aviation made very rapid progress and the experience gained in military flying proved very useful when the war was over. In June, 1919, flying a converted Vickers Vimy bomber, Alcock and Brown made the first non-stop flight over the North Atlantic and later that year Ross and Keith Smith flew from Britain to Australia.

Passenger Flying

Although these were both important steps in the acceptance of flying by the public, the birth of passenger flying as it is known today was in February, 1919, when the German airline Deutsche Luftreederei opened a service between Berlin, Leipzig and Weimar. In August of that year the first daily international commercial scheduled service was started by Aircraft Transport and Travel, Limited, which operated a de Havilland 4A. The fare charged on this pioneer route between London and Paris was £21 for a flight that lasted $2\frac{1}{2}$ hours.

The first transports to be used after the First World War were nearly all adapted bombers, machines like the Vickers Vimy commercial and the de Havilland DH9. Subsequently aircraft were designed from the beginning to carry passengers rather than bombs. In Germany Junkers, and in Holland Fokker, favoured the monoplane to the biplane, the former introducing the single-engined F–13 transport in 1919. This carried a crew of two and four passengers.

. In the following year the first successful large British transport, the Handley Page W.8, entered airline service; it carried 12 passengers. In 1925 the Ford Stout was introduced. This can be said to have been the first successful American airliner, for it cruised at 115 m.p.h. with 12 passengers. Two years later the first scheduled passenger service over the many existing United States mail routes was started by Colonial Air Transport, between New York and Boston.

Over the years, the major United States aircraft builders have produced many famous civil airliners, and in 1927, the same year that Lindbergh flew from New York to Paris to make the first solo Atlantic crossing, came the Lockheed Vega, a single-engined high-wing monoplane. It could carry a pilot and six passengers 900 miles at 135 m.p.h. While other countries were adopting the monoplane, Great Britain continued to design biplanes for commercial purposes. Such a policy, although backward looking, produced airliners as well known as the de Havilland Hercules and the Armstrong-Whitworth Argosy. Both were three-engined biplanes and were used on the Empire and European routes respectively of Imperial Airways.

Perhaps the best-known of all British

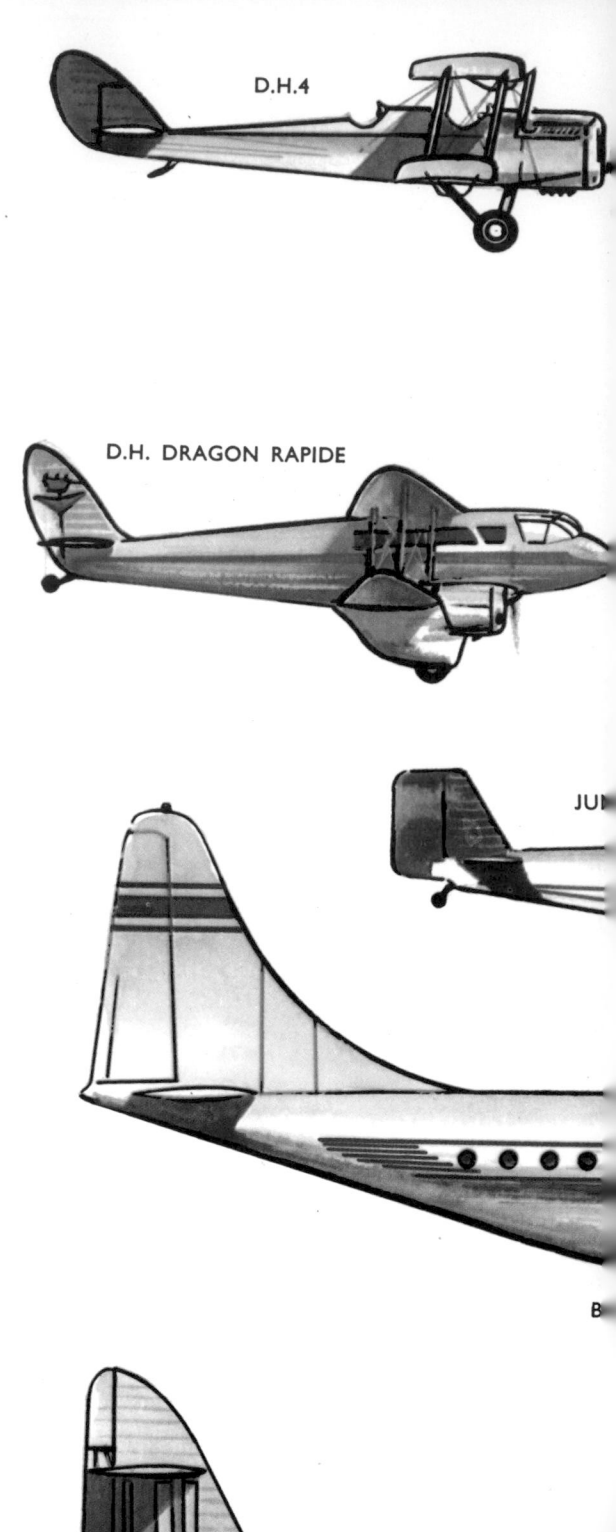

D.H.4

D.H. DRAGON RAPIDE

JU

B

DORNIER D.

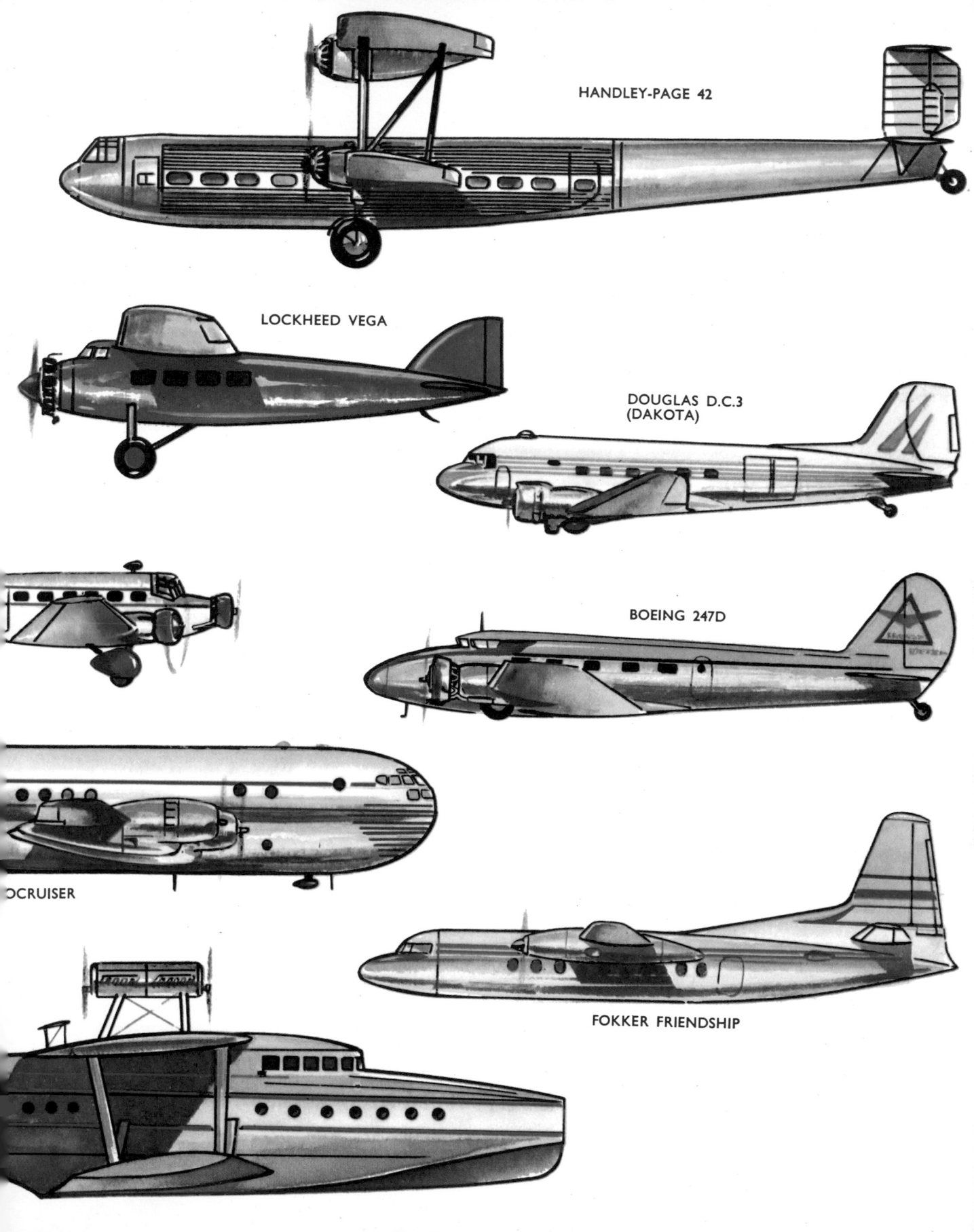

HANDLEY-PAGE 42

LOCKHEED VEGA

DOUGLAS D.C.3
(DAKOTA)

BOEING 247D

OCRUISER

FOKKER FRIENDSHIP

biplanes was the Handley Page HP42, known as the Hannibal on long-haul routes and the Heracles in European service. The Hannibal seated 24 and Heracles 38 passengers and both planes were powered by four Bristol Jupiter engines, entering Imperial Airways service in 1931.

This airline, which was Britain's main operator between the two world wars, introduced its first monoplane, the Armstrong-Whitworth Atalanta, the following year. In 1936 the company put its last new biplane into service, the four-engined de Havilland Diana. One of these attractive aircraft lasted throughout the war and was used by a private owner until 1958, when it was damaged beyond repair.

We have, however, jumped six or seven years and must return to the late 1920s. In Europe much of the work previously carried out in designing landplanes was being spent on the production of flying-boats.

During 1928 Short Brothers built the three-engined Calcutta, the first of a line of famous flying-boats that was later to include the Empire boats and the Sunderlands, and in Germany the following year the Dornier Company built the enormous Do. X. We shall return to flying-boats later, but no story of the development of civil aviation can ignore them, and Imperial Airways and Pan American Airways in particular were to use flying-boats to a considerable extent.

From flying-boats in Europe we must turn to the United States, where the modern airliner was born. In February, 1933, the Boeing 247 made its first flight and it was followed later that year by the

Douglas DC-1. Both these airliners had several major features that had not been included in earlier designs; among them were powerful supercharged radial engines mounted in the wings, a low-wing all-metal construction and a retractable undercarriage. The 247 carried 10 passengers and cruised at 155 m.p.h. It was introduced by United Air Lines on that company's coast-to-coast route across North America.

Only one DC-1 was built and it proved so promising that Douglas put a stretched version into production, the DC-2, which could carry 14 passengers. Having a cruising speed of 170 m.p.h. and a stage length of 350 miles, it was both faster and had a longer range than the Boeing 247. In December, 1935, the most famous transport plane ever made its first flight—the Douglas DC-3, better known as the Dakota. It was originally designed for American Airlines, which wanted a sleeper version of the DC-2 for use on the longer American internal routes. Production ceased in 1945, when over 13,000 DC-3s and similar machines had been built in Russia and Japan as well as in America—more than any other passenger aircraft. The Dakota can still be seen in all parts of the world.

In Europe, the most interesting aircraft of this period were being built by Fokker and Junkers. The Dutch designer Anthony Fokker was concentrating on trimotors—three-engined planes—among them the 14-passenger F.XVIII of 1932, which cruised at 155 m.p.h. Around the same time Junkers introduced the Ju 52/3m, also a three-engined aircraft, which carried 17 passengers at a cruising speed of about 130 m.p.h. The outstanding new British aircraft of this period, 1934, was the de Havilland 89A Dragon Rapide, developed from the Dragon of 1932. This robust little biplane was intended for short routes to serve as feeders for main or trunk services. British European Airways was still using Rapides on its Scilly Isles route in 1964, when they were replaced by helicopters. The Atalanta, already mentioned, was another land aircraft Britain produced at this time, but it was not the same quality as contemporary United States aircraft.

Before returning briefly to flying-boats, we should look at the Boeing 307 Stratoliner, which made its first flight in December, 1938. This was the first aircraft of the modern four-engined airliner type to enter service, being operated on long-haul United States internal routes. The Stratoliner carried 33 passengers and was the first airliner fitted with a pressurised cabin, enabling it to fly at high altitudes.

In 1936 the Short Empire class of flying-boats entered service with Imperial Airways, having been ordered the previous year while still in the design stage

A BEA D.H. Rapide flies over Land's End.

and before the first aircraft had flown. With a range of 800 miles and a cruising speed of 165 m.p.h. these four-engined monoplanes set a new standard of comfort for the 24 passengers they carried. It was from this aircraft that the famous wartime Sunderland was developed. In 1938 Boeing produced the 314, a flying-boat used by both Pan American and British Overseas Airways Corporation (BOAC), as the British long-distance airline was called after 1940.

During the Second World War the majority of the work carried out by the aircraft building industries was on military aircraft, although a few transport aircraft were designed. Of these the most important was the Douglas DC-4, also known as the Skymaster, which entered service with the United States armed forces in 1943. It was a four-engined aircraft which could carry 42 passengers for 1,500 miles at a speed of 200 m.p.h. Subsequently it was enlarged and modified to become the DC-6, which first flew in 1946.

Two other transport aircraft, both American, made their first flights before the war was over. One was the Lockheed Constellation, a most graceful four-engined plane with a triple fin. Carrying 51 passengers for more than 2,000 miles at 280 m.p.h., it was more comparable to the DC-6 than the DC-4. Another airliner was the Boeing Stratocruiser, which was developed from the famous B-29 Superfortress bomber. This was a "double deck aircraft" capable of carrying up to 100 passengers for 3,000 miles at 270 m.p.h. Some have recently been modified to carry sections of space rockets from California to Florida.

Following these aircraft came the new generation of airliners, powered by turbo-prop engines. The 320 m.p.h. Vickers Viscount, of which more than 400 were built, was introduced by British European Airways in 1953. It was the first short-haul turboprop aircraft. This was followed by, among others, the smaller and very successful twin-engined Fokker Friendship, built in Holland. For long-range service the only turboprop aircraft built in quantity were the Bristol Britannia and later the Russian Tupolev Tu-114 Rossiya, the jet engine proving itself to be more suitable for long-range work.

Jet Airliners

In May, 1952, British Overseas Airways Corporation introduced the world's first scheduled jet service, between London and Johannesburg, using de Havilland Comets. Since then, the greatest development in long-range jet aircraft has taken place in the United States, where the Boeing 707, the Douglas DC-8 and the Convair 880 and 990 have all been manufactured. Following the British Vickers VC-10 and the similar Ilyushin Il-62, which are the first second-generation long-range jets, will come supersonic airliners, mention of which will be made later.

The first short-range jet airliner was the French Sud Caravelle, which was also the first airliner to use rear-mounted jet engines. It was followed by the B.A.C. One-Eleven and the Trident, both British, and their American counterparts, respectively the Douglas DC-9 and Boeing 727. All four of these aircraft have tail-mounted engines.

Why an Aeroplane Flies

We have now covered, very briefly, the history of passenger aircraft up to around the present time, and before we look at the reasons for the new design layouts, it would be useful to consider the basic principles of aviation and see why an aircraft flies at all.

There are four main forces to be considered when seeing why an aeroplane flies—these are lift, speed, weight and drag, and we will look at each of them individually before seeing the effect on an aircraft they have together.

Aircraft fly because the air produces a force on anything moving through it and part of this force resists the object and tries to slow it down—as you know if you run fast against the wind. This force also tries to lift things and it is this that enables the aircraft to leave the ground. As the aircraft wing moves through the air there is a sucking effect on the top of the wing and pressure on the bottom. The lift of a wing depends upon three things—its shape, its angle to the wind and its speed through the air.

If the angle of the wing to the wind does not change—as it will if you raise or lower the nose of the aircraft—the lift varies as the square of the speed, so that if the aeroplane flies twice as fast the lift is four times as great; three times faster gives nine times the lift, and so on.

The nose of the aircraft is raised to give the wing the best angle for lift and there is a certain point when the lifting power of the wing is at its greatest. If it is lifted past that then the lifting power falls again. When this happens it means that the wing has stalled and the aircraft will fall like an ordinary weight, the lift

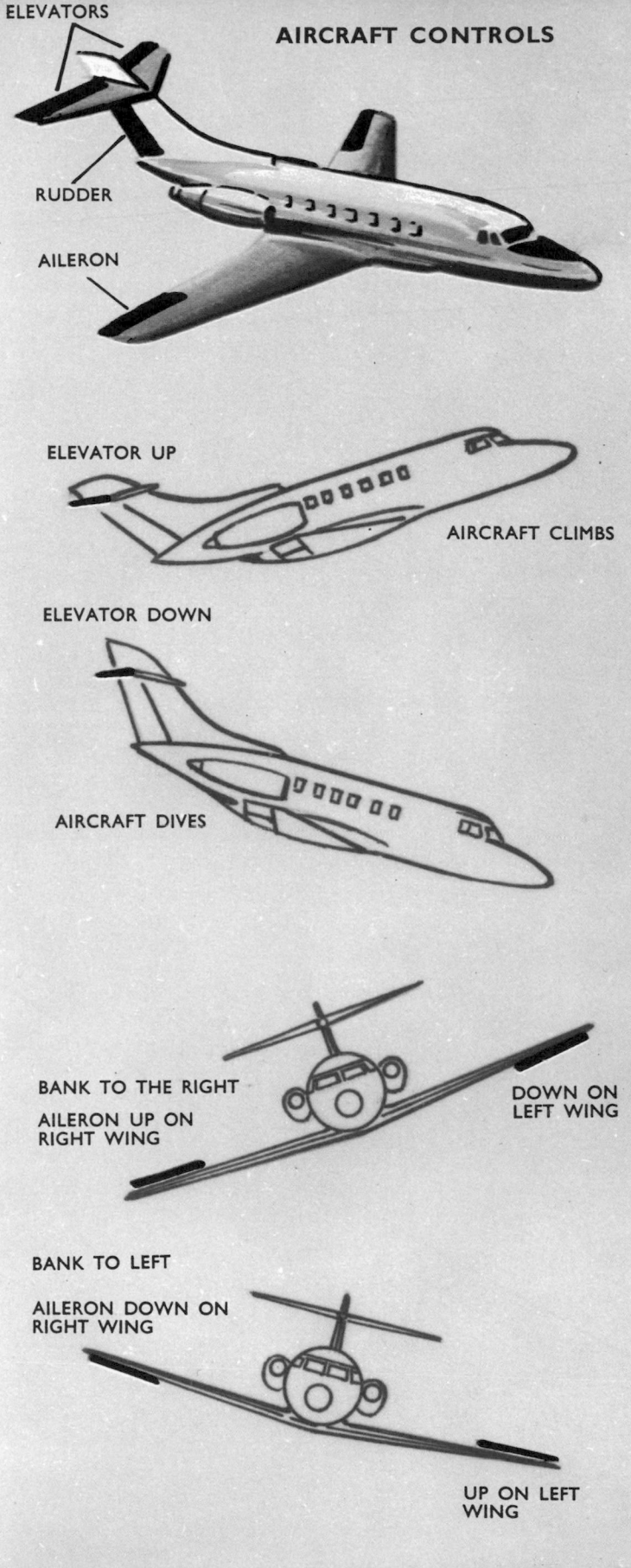

AIRCRAFT CONTROLS

ELEVATORS

RUDDER

AILERON

ELEVATOR UP

AIRCRAFT CLIMBS

ELEVATOR DOWN

AIRCRAFT DIVES

BANK TO THE RIGHT
AILERON UP ON RIGHT WING

DOWN ON LEFT WING

BANK TO LEFT
AILERON DOWN ON RIGHT WING

UP ON LEFT WING

not being enough to keep it flying. The speed of the aircraft is governed by the power of the engines, although the other three parts of the equation also have a considerable bearing on it.

That is a short account of speed and lift, which are the two positive parts of the simple equation—lift + speed = weight + drag—that shows how an aircraft flies. Now we must look at the two negative parts, weight and drag.

The lift of an aircraft, as we have seen, comes almost entirely from the wings, and very little from the fuselage and the other parts of the aircraft. The drag from the wings however, is almost non-existent when compared with that from the rest of the aircraft. We have seen that a wing exerts lift only because it is moved through the air, and that there is a force trying to stop the movement. This force is known as drag, or resistance.

The fourth factor is weight, and this acts vertically downwards in the same way that the lift acts upwards. Therefore, when an aircraft is flying level the lift is equal to the weight; if the lift were more than the weight the aircraft would rise, and if it were less it would descend.

Controlling an Aeroplane

Having looked briefly at the four factors that go to make up the theory of why aeroplanes fly, we will now turn to the main controls that give an aeroplane the ability to change its height and course. There are four main controls—the rudder, the ailerons, the elevators and flaps.

The aileron is a hinged control surface on the trailing edge of each wing, usually near the tip. The operation of the ailerons causes one wing to lift, the other

to drop; they are usually used in connection with the rudder to enable the aircraft to bank as it turns, although the aircraft could make a flat skidding turn on the rudder only. The elevator is a hinged horizontal structure in the aircraft's tail to govern an aircraft's ascent or descent. The rudder is operated by pedals and the elevator and ailerons by the control column. The flaps, controlled by a wheel or lever in the cockpit, are, like the ailerons, mounted on the trailing edge of the wing, usually near the fuselage. The flaps, when lowered, increase the air resistance and so slow the aircraft down; this is particularly useful for landing.

In addition to these basic controls, modern high-speed aircraft are fitted with slots, a safety device fitted on the leading edge of the wing to delay the stalling of an aircraft. They also enable level control to be maintained after the theoretical point of stall has been passed.

How Aeroplanes are Built

Now that we have taken a very brief look at how an aeroplane flies and is controlled, we can turn back and follow the design and construction of a modern airliner. The design of aircraft today is a result of much research. It is not surprising, then, to find that many aircraft designed for similar tasks look alike—thus the Trident looks like the Boeing 727 and the Boeing 707 like the Douglas DC-8.

The first thing a company designing an airliner must consider is its market—it must find this out by asking airlines the range, the speed and the passenger capacity they want. Once this is done the design team can start designing an aircraft to meet the specification. The designers

The final assembly line for the BAC One-Eleven at Hurn.

must decide on the right number of engines to give the aircraft the most economical performance, and where they should be mounted; whether or not to sweep the wings back; where to position the strengthening spars, and the size of the fuselage. Many smaller points have also to be considered, such as the siting of doors, the layout of the cockpit and the size of the landing wheels.

Once these points have been decided upon, the manufacturer builds a wooden mock-up of the aircraft; this enables potential purchasers of the aircraft to see exactly what it will look like. It also helps the manufacturers to make final decisions on the layout of the cockpit and the passenger cabin.

Once the company has decided on the layout of the airliner it is to build, it has to design every piece of the aircraft, from the smallest nut to the largest wing panels. First the major parts, such as the strengthening spars in the wing, and then the smaller components, are designed and ordered. The main components are assembled into major units, such as the outer part of the wing and the nose of the fuselage. Various parts of the aircraft may be made at different factories or even, as in the case of the Concord supersonic airliner, in different countries.

The major units are assembled into a complete aircraft in an assembly shop where the major systems of the aircraft, such as the brakes and the gear for raising and lowering the landing wheels, are also fitted. These systems are given a thorough test first, and the landing gear will undergo a series of several hundred simulated lowerings and raisings in a few days. The last components are fitted and the aircraft is complete.

Before the aircraft flies, however, the engines are tested on the ground at varying powers and then the aircraft is taxied round the airfield to see how it handles on the ground. Then slow, and later fast, taxi trials are carried out on the runway. Finally the aircraft makes its first flight, some two or three years after work has started on it.

Even now the aircraft does not enter service. In his first flights the test pilot gets the feel of the aircraft and then carries out development flying, the day-to-day work on testing the aircraft in flight that is needed to obtain a Certificate of Airworthiness which every aircraft has to have before it can carry passengers in airline service. This development flying period involves the testing of the aircraft in both normal and unusual attitudes, and includes stall tests and flying with one or more engines out of action.

As more aircraft are built they will join the prototype on the development flying programme. One aircraft will carry out trials in the tropics and at airfields at a considerable altitude, to ensure that the power on the engines, which decreases in both these cases, is still satisfactory. Later on, passengers are carried on trial flights, and finally flights are made on the airline's routes to see how it behaves in everyday service. When all these tests have been carried out, and the many small snags that beset any new airliner are remedied, the aircraft will receive its Certificate of Airworthiness and enter passenger service.

Modern Airliner Design

We have briefly surveyed the stages of bringing an airliner into production and now we can turn to some of the features of the modern airliner and see why it looks

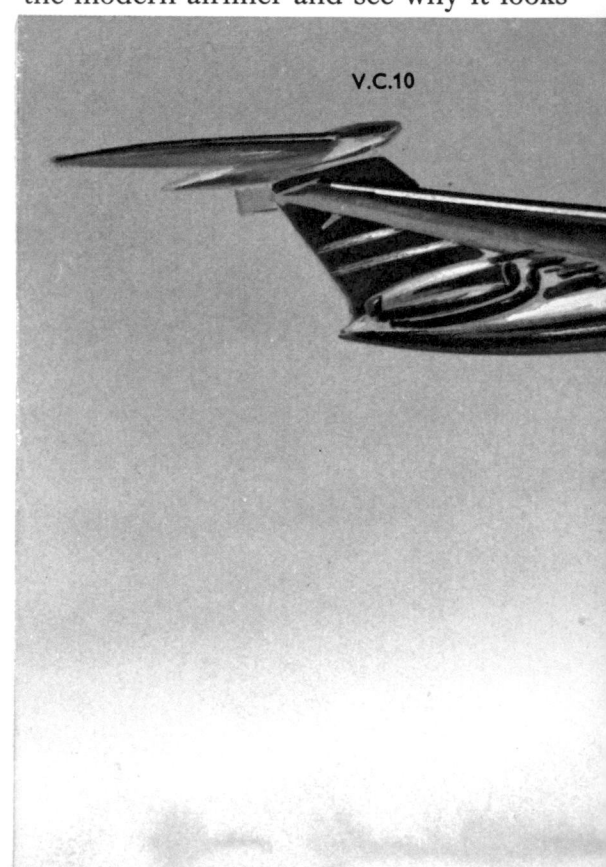

V.C.10

the way it does. When we were looking at the principles of flight it was seen that to reduce drag to a minimum the shape of the aeroplane had to be as sleek as possible. This has always been so, especially in fighter aircraft.

In the same way that a bus is merely a box on wheels, so the fuselage of the aircraft is a cigar with wings. It has to be streamlined and there has not been much advance in the actual shape of the fuselage since the end of the Second World War—the Trident fuselage is not so distant in appearance from that of the DC-4 as are other parts of the aircraft.

Every advance in aircraft design is aimed at improving one of several features of an airliner—it will make it fly faster, or further, or with more people or more economically. The Douglas DC-7C was developed from the earlier DC-7B, having a 10 ft. extension

at the wing roots and a 40 in. fuselage extension. The DC-7C was the last of the long family of Douglas propeller-driven transports, each of which was an enlarged version of its predecessor. It is, however, a great advance from the 21-passenger 190 m.p.h. twin-engined DC-3 to its logical development, the 99-passenger 345 m.p.h. four-engined DC-7C.

Although modern airliners can also be stretched, as the VC10 became the Super VC10 with a two-deck development—the Superb—planned, but later cancelled, they keep their basic characteristics. Therefore, all the VC10 family have four tail-mounted engines, a high tail and swept wings. Looking at these one at a time, let us start with the position of engines in the modern jet airliner.

In early jets, such as the Tupolev Tu 104 and the Comet, the engines are mounted in the wing roots, a position which

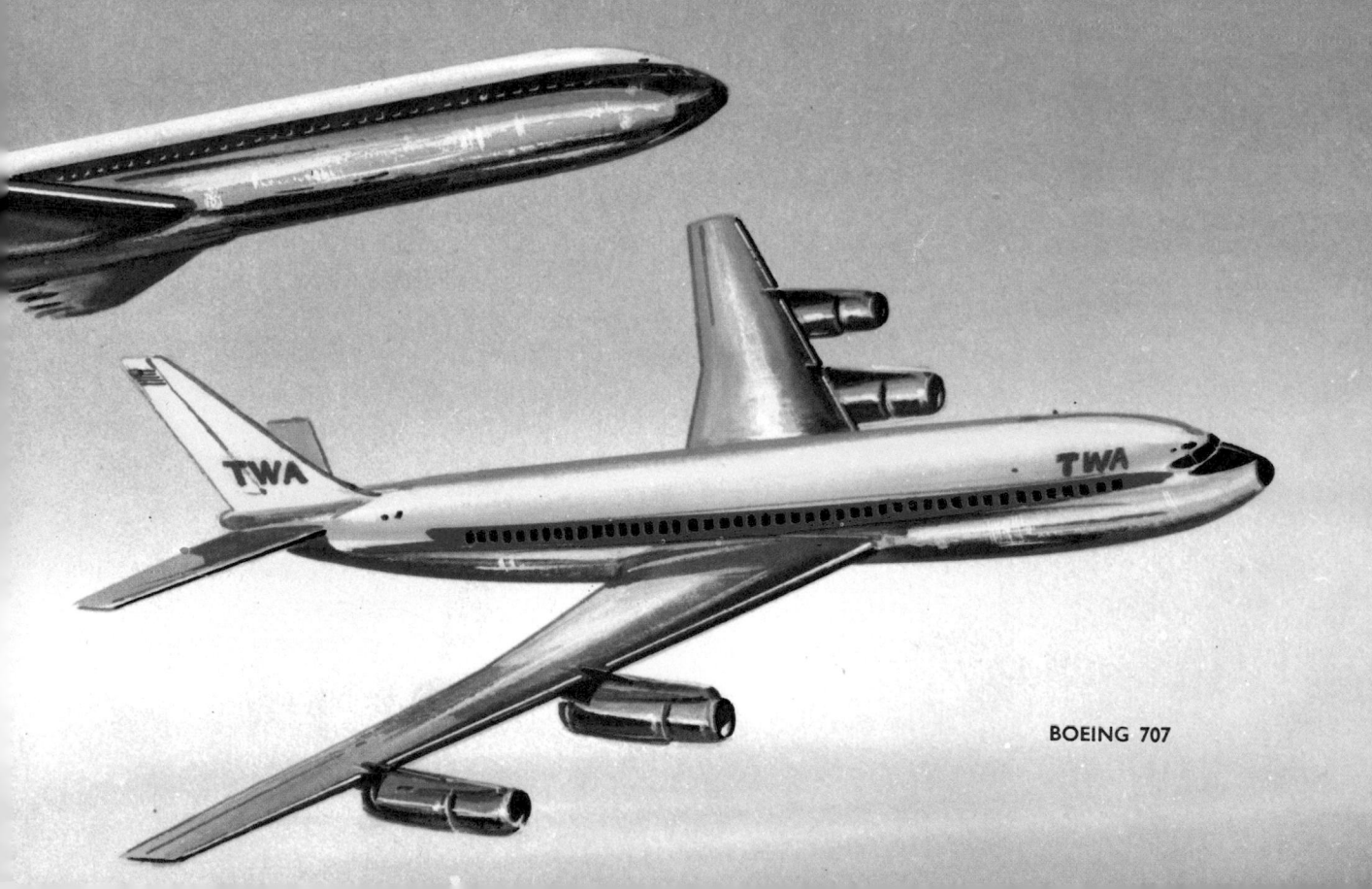

BOEING 707

suffered from two main disadvantages, that the maintenance was not easy and that the wing had to be strengthened and widened to accommodate them. The next position, in aircraft such as the Boeing 707 and the Convair 880, was in pods under the wings. This simplified the maintenance, but the wing still had to be strengthened to support the weight of the engines. There are other disadvantages with this layout, including the additional drag caused by the bulky engine being slung below the wing.

The layout favoured at present is for the engines to be externally mounted at the tail of the aircraft, with the third engine, in the case of three-engined machines like the Trident and Boeing 727, mounted at the base of the tailplane. This makes maintenance comparatively easy and has two other big advantages; it leaves the wing free of any other duties apart from its main one of providing lift, and it means that should one of the engines fail in flight there will be less tendency for the aircraft to swing away in the opposite direction since the remaining thrust is much nearer the centre line of the aircraft.

We shall look at jet and turboprop engines later, but it should be noted here that with piston and turboprop engines, both of which drive propellers, nearly all multi-engined aircraft have their engines mounted in the wing. It is only with the jet engine, with which there is no need for clearance for the arc of the propeller, that it has been possible to mount the engines as near the passenger cabin as they are in the Comet and the Caravelle.

The next thing to look at is the shape of the wing. In piston-engined aircraft the wings usually tapered slowly and sometimes the trailing edge of the wing was almost at right-angles to the fuselage. As speeds increased, however, this layout proved to be inefficient so swept and delta wings were developed. Both of these have the same advantage over straighter wings, in that they give a lot of lift at comparatively low landing speeds and also the best possible performance at maximum speeds.

A high tail-mounting on a modern aircraft gives it better handling, as the control surfaces, being above the air disturbed by the passage of the rest of the aircraft, are flying through "new" air. As there is no turbulence in this the control surfaces are able to "grip" the air better and thus the elevators and rudder are more effective. This, too, is a direct result of higher speeds, for with slower aircraft their passage caused less disturbance of the air and the position of the tailplane was of less importance.

Freight Aircraft

With freight aircraft the problems are different for speeds are, on the whole, not so important, although cargo-carrying versions of passenger airliners, such as the Boeing 707–320C and the Douglas DC–8F, are in service with many airlines. The main essential for all modern freighters is easy and quick loading, although speed of delivery is a great asset of airfreighting.

The later piston-engined freighters and many of the present jets are fitted with large side-doors behind the cockpit or in front of the tail unit through which freight can be loaded. These, however, suffer the disadvantage that any freight that is bulkier than the size of the door cannot be loaded. There are two ways by which this problem can be overcome—by having entry either through the nose or through the tail.

The conventional way of doing this is by giving the aircraft a higher tail and loading through a hinged ramp into the rear of the fuselage, a layout that is used in the Lockheed Hercules. A variation on this idea is to have the tail mounted on booms, leaving the rear of the fuselage free. This is the layout adopted in the Hawker Siddeley Argosy, although with this aircraft there is yet another refinement, for the nose also hinges—the cockpit being set above the cargo compartment—enabling loading and unloading to take place simultaneously, one at each end.

One of the most ingenious answers to the problems of loading is the Canadian swing-tail, all-cargo aircraft, the Canadair CL–44. In this aircraft the whole of the tail unit swings round to one side to allow direct loading of cargo into the tail of the aircraft. The main advantage of this type of aircraft is that one long piece of equipment, providing that it is not too wide or too high, can be loaded easily, while an aircraft with a conventional cargo door would not be able to receive it.

Helicopters

Helicopters have a very bright future, for they can carry out tasks that are beyond the capabilities of ordinary aircraft.

Two Sikorsky Helicopters
Above right: A BEA S61-N taking off with passengers.
Right: A helicopter designed to carry military and commercial vehicles.

The first real helicopter was designed and built during the 1930s, but the idea of a flying machine with a wing that rotates goes back to Leonardo da Vinci. The helicopter is developed from the gyrodine, a type of aircraft made popular in the 1930s by Cierva, which had a rotor to give it lift, and an ordinary propeller for forward travel. This rotor was driven by the engine when the gyrodine was climbing and "windmilled" in level flight and when descending. The main disadvantage of the gyrodine was that it could not hover or move sideways; in fact the only real advantage that it had over a

normal aircraft was that it did not need an airfield for take-off and landing.

A helicopter has no propeller at the front as a gyrodine had, but is driven through the rotor which is tilted according to the direction of travel; if the pilot wishes the machine to fly to the left he tilts the rotor to the left, as can be seen from the accompanying diagram. The small rotor at the tail is to counteract the tendency of a helicopter to spin in the opposite direction to the rotor, a feature known as torque.

Most of the early work in developing helicopters was done in the United States, the Bell 47 being the first machine to be granted a licence for civil flying. By 1947, both Britain and France had built and flown helicopters and other countries had developed practical designs, although they had not flown.

In the 1950s experimental services were begun in Britain and in Europe, where the Belgian state airline, Sabena, introduced the first international helicopter services. These services did not make a profit and the British services were withdrawn and some of the European routes were also taken off. Helicopters at that time were too slow, too small and too expensive to operate and compete with other forms of transport.

Bigger and more economic helicopters were developed and now there are helicopter services operated by airlines throughout the world. The most interesting is in East Pakistan, where the mountain ranges and rivers make land travel very difficult, and a two-hour helicopter journey might take two days by land. Another use of the helicopter today is serving islands—Capri and Ischia in the

Mediterranean and the Isles of Scilly off Cornwall all have helicopter services.

In Melbourne and Moscow helicopters are used almost as taxis, flying between the city centre and the main airport. In the United States there are helicopter airlines running regular, if not always profitable, services in Chicago, Los Angeles, New York and San Francisco.

These are the transport aspects of helicopters, but there are many other fields in which they are employed. Among the military uses are carrying troops, hunting and killing submarines and acting as air-sea rescue machines; all tasks which they can carry out better than a fixed-wing aircraft because of their special ability to hover and to land in a small area.

In civilian activities as well as military it is the ability to hover and to land in a restricted space that enables the helicopter to carry out many of the tasks it does so well. In California, helicopters are used to spot forest fires, in the Middle East to supply oil derricks at sea, and everywhere to act as cranes or to patrol power lines.

There are two lines of research and development that the aircraft manufacturers are at present following for building the next generations of transports—supersonic airliners and machines which are able to take-off and land vertically. The latter, which are usually known as V.T.O.L. aircraft, are a logical development of the gyrodine and the helicopter and are under development in many countries.

The most advanced design is the British Hawker Kestrel, a ground-attack fighter. This is powered by a single jet

A Sikorsky S61 helicopter airliner of Pakistan
International Airways in flight. Machines
such as these are ideal for carrying passengers
over areas of forest and rivers where other
forms of transport would be difficult or
impossible to use.

A SIKORSKY S61 HELICOPTER AIRLINER

engine, the exhaust nozzles for which can be rotated so that they point either downwards for vertical or rearwards for normal flying, swivelling in flight for the transition stage.

Another system of V.T.O.L. operation is to have separate engines for lift and forward flight, but this system is not yet as advanced. A third system is one that is used mainly for propeller-driven aircraft, such as the experimental Canadair Dynavert, and involves the tilting of the whole wing through a right-angle. By positioning the wing at an intermediate angle, the Dynavert can take-off in a very short distance, while carrying a greater payload than it can as a V.T.O.L. aircraft.

Faster than Sound

Work is also progressing in Britain, France, Russia and the United States on the Concord and other supersonic transports. The Concord, which is being built jointly by Britain and France, seems most likely to fly first. The target date is early 1968 and it should enter service four years later. Construction is in hand at Bristol and Toulouse. There is no duplication of production, however; the building of the various assemblies is being divided between the two centres before transportation to the appropriate country for final assembly.

There will be two versions of the Concord produced, both cruising at about 1,450 m.p.h., or nearly two and a quarter times the speed of sound, at a height of more than 50,000 ft. The main difference is one of range, one type being able to fly around 2,800 miles non-stop and the other, enlarged, type around 4,000 miles.

In Russia a supersonic airliner with a similar cruising speed is being built.

The Concord and the Russian model were, until recently, the only two firm supersonic projects.

In America nothing was certain. Both Lockheed and Boeing submitted designs to the government for supersonic transports. The Lockheed CL - 823 was designed to carry 220 passengers at over 2,000 m.p.h. between London and New York. The other design, the Boeing 733, would carry 150 passengers at about 1,800 m.p.h., although an enlarged version carrying more than 220 passengers has been proposed.

Because of the very high cost of development it was always certain that only one of the two would be built and go into airline service. The Boeing was recently chosen as the American rival to the Concord. It will have variable wings that fold back into a dart shape for high-speed flight and swing forward for landing and taking-off and when flying below the speed of sound.

Flying-Boats and Airships

Having looked at the present and the future of aircraft design, it would be useful, before moving on to present-day operating methods, to look at two lines of aircraft design that have been abandoned. These are flying-boats and airships.

The first successful airship flight was made by Henri Giffard, who flew the 17 miles from Paris to Trappes in 1852, and by the turn of the century airships had, despite many setbacks, become accepted. In 1900, the first of Count Zeppelin's airships, LZ. 1, flew, and between 1910 and 1914 passenger services operated in

Germany. Although three Zeppelins were destroyed, no passenger or crew member was hurt. After the First World War, in which lighter-than-air craft proved themselves extremely useful, a lot of development went into airships, especially in Britain and Germany, and in 1919 the British airship R.34 crossed the Atlantic to make both the first east-to-west and the first return crossing by air.

In 1926 the airship *Norge* was used on an Arctic exploration and two years later the *Italia* was lost on a similar expedition. The years between the two world wars were, in fact, punctuated by a series of airship accidents, but the majority of these were due either to the lack of weather forecasting or to the bad design of the airships. Most of these accidents would not have happened to an airship of modern design.

Against the succession of accidents must be set the success of the German airship *Graf Zeppelin*—scrapped in 1937—which flew more than a million miles in about 650 flights—144 of them across the Atlantic—and carried more

than 18,000 passengers successfully. This airship was the most successful commercial lighter-than-air craft ever built, and during the nine years that she was in service she did more to popularise the idea of airships than any other single craft.

At present there are very few airships in service, although the United States Navy has two squadrons of blimps, as non-rigid airships are often called, in service at Lakehurst, New Jersey. There is, however, a considerable amount of pressure being exerted at present towards the building of airships for certain purposes. It would bridge the gap in speed between the aircraft and the ship, having the comfort of the latter because of its large lifting power. Because of their very large fuel tanks airships can hover longer than a helicopter and, with the greater lifting ability already mentioned, could carry out tasks that would take too long or be outside the capacity of the helicopter.

Despite the fact that the airship is decried and written off by most people, it is still a most useful type of transport. It has its limitations, as have all forms of transport, but for certain functions it could, even now, prove extremely useful.

The flying-boat has already been mentioned in the general historical summary, but it is too important a development to be mentioned merely in passing. Flying-boats were used during the First World War, although in commercial flying the earlier use of the Benoist flying-boat between Tampa and St. Petersburg in 1914 has already been remarked upon.

The two most famous names in the history of flying-boats are Short Brothers and Imperial Airways, the builders and operators of the Empire class and many other flying-boats. The first Short boat operated by the British airline was the Calcutta of 1928, to be followed by the Scipio and by the Empire class in 1933.

The C class, as the Empire boats were also called, carried 24 passengers and the range was eventually extended to 2,500 miles. It was from the C class that the famous Sunderland was developed. Very little development was carried on outside Britain and the United States, where the very successful Sikorsky flying-boats were built in the 1930s, although the German 12-engined Dornier Do. X could carry 169 passengers over 1,900 miles.

One interesting experiment with flying-boats was carried out in the 1930s with the Short Mayo composite aircraft, which was a seaplane mounted on the upper wing of an Empire class flying-boat. The flying-boat then took off, its payload being the seaplane which, not having to carry the fuel to take-off and climb to its operating height, could operate over a greater distance. *Mercury*,

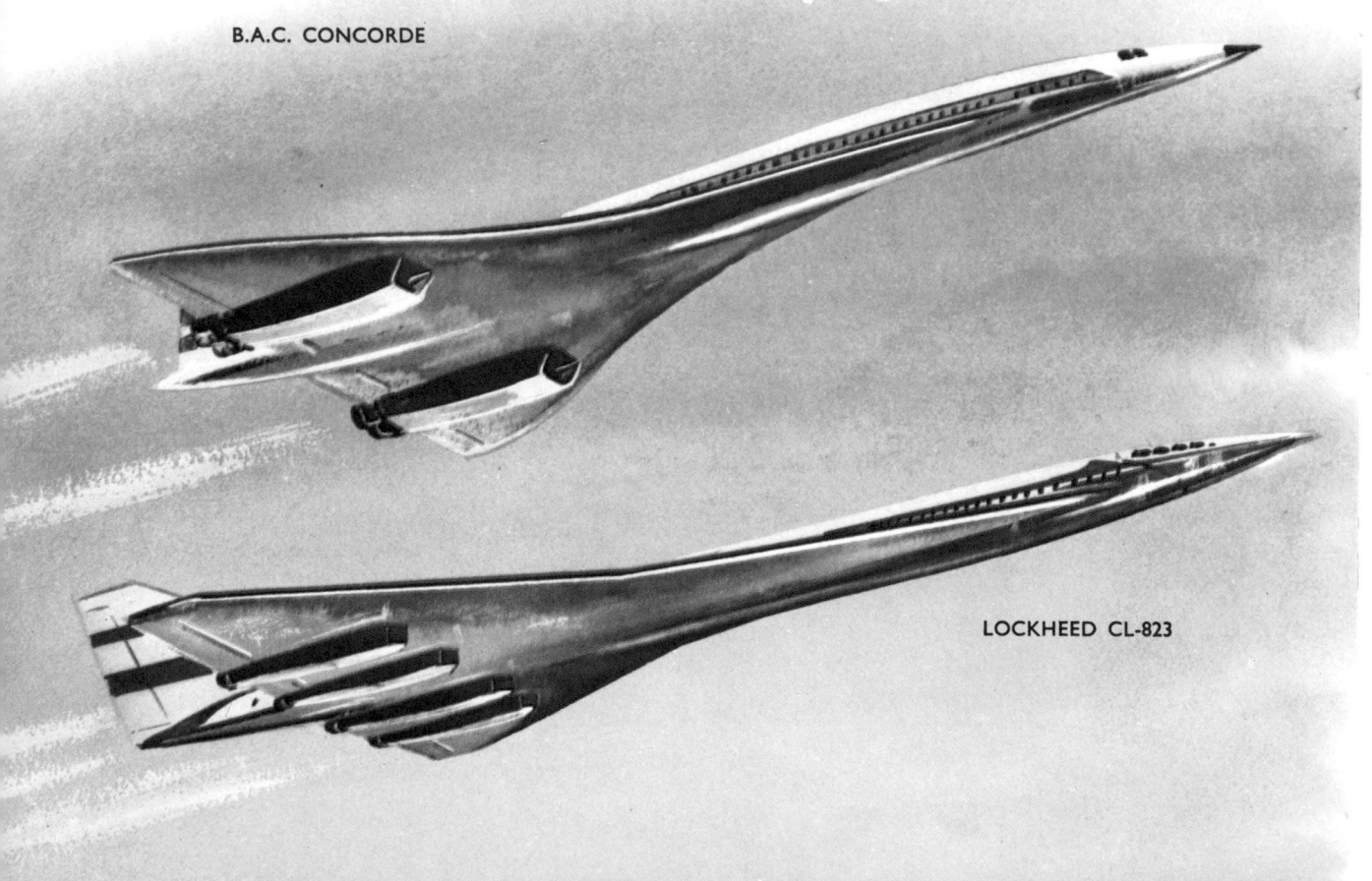

B.A.C. CONCORDE

LOCKHEED CL-823

GRAF ZEPPELIN COMPARED TO A FOKKER TRI-MOTOR AIRLINER OF THE SAME PERIOD

as the upper component was called, made a transatlantic flight in July, 1938, but the project was cancelled even though it had proved itself to be feasible.

After the Empire class came the Short G class and the American Boeing 314, the latter being used extensively by Pan American Airways and also by BOAC. After the Second World War most airlines decided to operate land-based aircraft as they were more economic than comparable flying-boats. British Overseas Airways Corporation was the last airline to operate flying-boats on trunk routes, operating Short Solents between Britain and South Africa until 1949. One place in which flying-boats are still used today is on the Amazon where a regular service is operated by a Brazilian airline.

The last British flying-boat to be designed was the Saunders Roe Princess, three of which were started but only one flew, although without the engines origi-nally designed for it, and even this was soon stored. Perhaps the last word in modern flying-boat construction is the Martin Seamaster, a four-jet reconnaissance aircraft for the United States Navy. This has a maximum speed of 630 m.p.h. and a normal range of 1,500 miles with a payload of 30,000 lb.

Commercially there seems to be very little future for the large flying-boat, although seaplanes—aircraft with floats instead of wheels—are used for transport in countries with many lakes, such as Canada, and as bush transport.

Maintaining an Aircraft

Just as every aircraft is built to a great degree of accuracy and has to be thoroughly flight tested before it receives its Certificate of Airworthiness, it has to undergo regular maintenance. All the major airlines have their own base for this purpose—like those of Air Canada

123

British Aircraft Corporation's One-Eleven being assembled.

at Winnipeg and Montreal, or of BEA at London Airport.

Every flight is recorded in logbooks, and separate logbooks are kept for the engines and the aircraft, in addition to that which the pilot must keep. In these all details of repairs and inspections are entered. After a set number of hours—more than a thousand hours for some well-proved engines—the engines are taken out of the aircraft and given a thorough overhaul. For example, BOAC runs its own engine overhaul base in South Wales in addition to the aircraft maintenance base at London Airport.

Besides these overhauls, every aircraft must receive a daily Certificate of Airworthiness from a licensed ground engineer before it can fly passenger services. This is in addition to the main Certificate which is renewed annually after a thorough inspection.

How a Jet Motor Works

Having mentioned engines and their maintenance, the time has now come to see how a jet motor works. The simplest form is a ramjet, in which paraffin or some other fuel is burnt and the hot gases allowed to escape from a nozzle at the rear of the combustion chamber. It is the reaction of the jet exhaust on the surrounding air that causes the aircraft to move forward—the greater the air stream from the rear of the engine the greater the forward thrust.

An aircraft needs a lot of thrust to propel it, and to obtain the large volume of gas to give this thrust it is necessary to burn a substantial amount of fuel quickly, and this in turn requires a large amount of oxygen in which to burn. To give it this oxygen a compressor is mounted in front of the combustion chamber to compress the large amount of air needed. The hot gases that result from the combustion drive a gas turbine before passing out through the tail nozzle, and it is this turbine which powers the compressor. The turbine and the compressor take some of the power from the hot gases, which means that there is that much less power to provide forward thrust; without these two parts, however, the engine would not be able to burn the fuel quickly enough.

Most modern jet aircraft are powered by by-pass engines, also known as turbo-fans—such as the Spey, three of which power the Hawker Siddeley Trident. This engine develops a thrust of 10,400 lb. at sea-level, and works on the same principle as the ordinary jet engine with one major difference, that not all the air goes through the combustion chamber.

In the Spey there are two compressors, all the air passing through the first, which is a low-pressure compressor. Some of the air is then diverted away and thus by-passes the high-pressure compressor and the combustion chamber. This arrangement is more economic than the traditional jet motor, as it gives a low fuel consumption for the amount of thrust developed. A further advantage is that the outer stream of cool air helps to quieten the roar caused by the hot gases leaving the engine.

A turboprop engine is an ordinary jet engine but with a propeller mounted on the front of the shaft carrying the compressor and the turbine. It is used on air-craft cruising around 400 to 550 m.p.h. flying slower than the jet and also at a lower height, to give a compromise between the jet and the normal propeller-driven aircraft. The piston engine is, as the name suggests, a normal internal-combustion engine, and turboprop engines are now being installed instead of the piston engine in all but the smallest new aircraft.

Airline Journeys

The normal airline flight is much the same, whether the journey is from Sydney to Singapore in a Boeing 707 of Qantas Empire Airways or from Glasgow to the Western Isles in a BEA Viscount. The length and the comfort of the journey vary, but the principle is the same.

There are, however, several types of air journey that differ completely from the normal pattern, usually because of their terminal points and the traffic between them. These are more interesting than the ordinary journeys because they show how air travel can adapt itself to meet the needs of people, and it is people who matter. For instance, there are two interesting services to take people across the English Channel—the "Silver Arrow", which is the air equivalent of the more famous "Golden Arrow" boat and train journey between London and Paris, and a service operated by Skyways Coach Air. In both cases the aircraft flies only about a third of the distance between the two capitals, the outside sectors being operated by rail and coach respectively.

In the United States a similar situation exists where a large number of people wish to travel between certain large

Above: Chicago Airport; showing the neat docking arrangement.
Below: A TU-124 Russian turbojet airliner at Sheremetyevo Airport.

cities. Here the traffic is so heavy that Eastern Air Lines operates a regular service between New Orleans and Houston without there being any of the formalities that one normally associates with airline journeys. A passenger arrives at the airport and walks aboard the aircraft without any reservation; he buys his ticket in flight. If the aircraft is full the airline will run another. Similar services are flown between certain other American cities, including the air-bus service between New York and Washington.

These arrangements are typical of the variety of service that are being operated by the airlines. Other inducements are also being offered by airlines to attract passengers. These cannot be financial, for all fares are fixed by international agreement, an organisation known as the International Air Transport Association regulating fares on all the international routes. They therefore have to offer special services.

Certain international airlines, for example, show a full-length film on long-distance flights, the film chosen being

A BEA Trident at London Airport.

A BEA Trident airliner in flight.

changed regularly. Other airlines seek to win passengers by the quality of the food they offer. In the United States, American Airlines try to gain more passengers by showing television programmes in flight—either showing the scenery over which the aircraft is flying or else relaying programmes sent out by the stations in the area.

Stewards and stewardesses have been a feature of travel by air since the early 1920s, when an early British operator, Daimler Airways, took on three cabin boys. Another British airline, Imperial Airways, first employed stewards with similar functions to those at sea, in 1927. These stewards served light snacks to passengers and when the airline introduced the Handley Page Hannibal seven-course meals were served.

Meals are served today on the majority of long-distance flights and on many shorter journeys as well. Most airliners have kitchens for preparing food for use when the aircraft is airborne. The stew-

ards and stewardesses who serve the food, among their other duties, are all specially trained and are capable of dealing with many emergencies, from a passenger taken ill in flight to the more routine matter of a missing passport.

Although an airline operates cargo and charter passenger services, its main source of revenue still comes from the regular flights. Nearly every city and major town throughout the world is now served by a scheduled airline service. Early air services were operated between the big cities—from London to Paris or from New York to Washington—because the larger the centres of population at the terminals the greater the chance of carrying enough passengers to make the services pay.

From this type of route, efforts were made to link major cities that lie much further apart—such as London and Cape Town, which were linked by an Imperial Airways through service in 1932. The service was flown in many short sections,

The interior of a Boeing 707. The stewardess is adjusting one of the television screens which show films during a flight.

the 8,000 mile flight taking 10½ days. Long flights over water came later, when aircraft had the ability to fly such distances without having to land to refuel. The first fare-paying air passengers to cross the North Atlantic apart from those in airships were carried by Pan American Airways in the summer of 1939, using flying-boats.

After the Second World War people became more aware of the advantages of travelling by air. Air fares dropped and people were soon able to afford to fly on pleasure as well as business trips. This led to services being flown not only to the major cities, but also to tourist centres. Therefore there are today flights from Britain to towns such as Alicante in the south of Spain—a centre for tourists rather than business men. Another feature of this awareness of the advantages of flying is inclusive tours; the traveller makes one payment to cover his flight to a centre, his coach to his hotel and his hotel itself. These services are mainly operated at night, when the aircraft

would probably not otherwise be used, and the cost of the whole tour is usually about the same as for the air fare on a regular scheduled service.

Another feature of air transport that has developed since the end of the Second World War is the introduction of local-service airlines. These serve a fairly large area and act as feeders to the major operators, and both the United States and Australia have several such airlines. Typical examples would be Trans-Texas Airways, which serves six southern central American states, and East-West Airlines, which operates in New South Wales and southern Queensland. They provide a local service inside the area they serve and also funnel people to the major cities to join long and medium-distance flights. The major advantage of this type of airline is that because its costs are lower it can operate to towns that it would not pay a trunk airline to serve.

Before leaving passenger flying, it would be interesting to look briefly at the work that goes on before an airline

Interior of the cockpit of a
Trident airliner.

Carrying Freight

Earlier on we looked at freight aircraft and saw how they differed from passenger aircraft and why this had come about. Now we can look at the growth of freight transport by air and also at certain special types of freight that are carried by air today.

The cargo carried on the first international service, across the English Channel in 1919, included grouse and Devonshire cream; since then the variety of freight carried has widened considerably. Mail was one of the first cargoes to be carried regularly by air, and many of the United States airlines are descended from the mail carriers of the 1920s—thus United Air Lines is a direct successor of Varney Air Lines that began operation in 1926.

There was a similar situation in Europe. In 1919 the British airline, Aircraft Transport and Travel, was granted a six-month monopoly for carrying official mail between London and Paris. The British Government encouraged the use of air transport for carrying the mail, and two years later an air service for the mail was started across the desert between Egypt and Ramadi, near Baghdad. In 1931 an airmail service was opened between England and Australia.

It should not be thought, however, that all the early cargo was mail, although

operates a new service. First of all the airline, for commercial reasons, satisfies itself that there is a demand for the service. Should it be necessary, the company then gets the approval of its Government to operate the service. If the route is an international one, agreement will then have to be reached between the two Governments on such points as the frequency of the service. The airline would then operate several proving flights to enable the captains to learn the layout of the new airport and to discover any special features about the route. When all these matters have been settled passenger services can be started.

An American Airlines Astrojet in flight.

AUTOMATIC LANDING

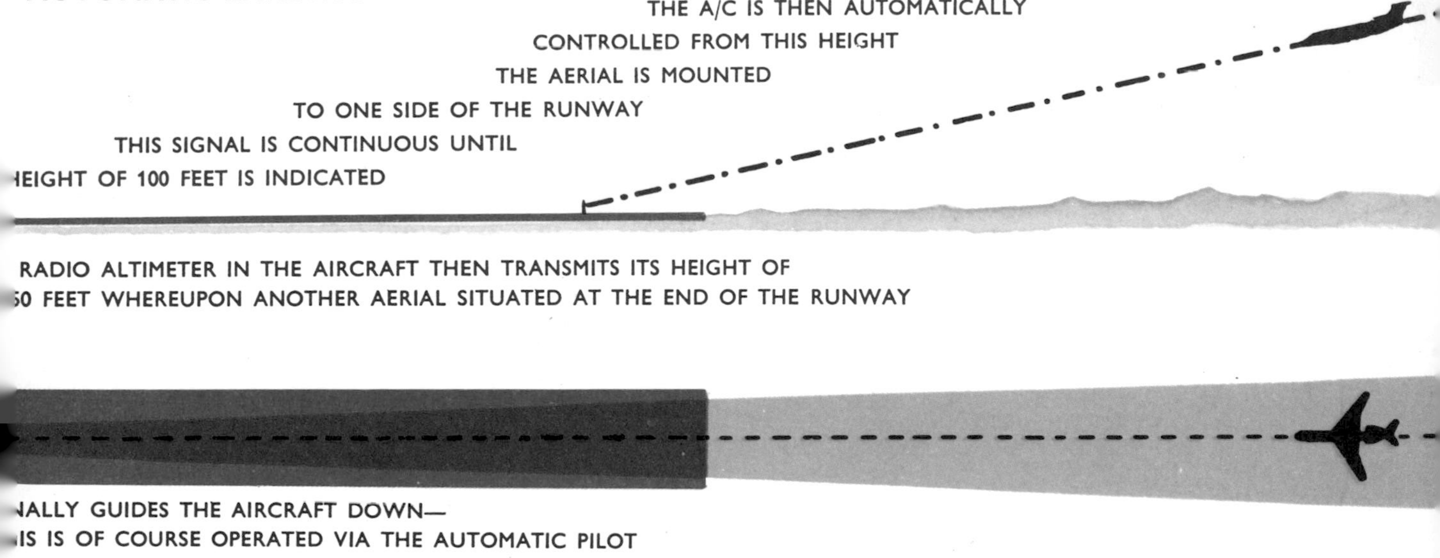

GLIDE PATH SIGNAL
BECOMES EFFECTIVE AT
1,200 FEET

THE A/C IS THEN AUTOMATICALLY
CONTROLLED FROM THIS HEIGHT
THE AERIAL IS MOUNTED
TO ONE SIDE OF THE RUNWAY
THIS SIGNAL IS CONTINUOUS UNTIL
HEIGHT OF 100 FEET IS INDICATED

RADIO ALTIMETER IN THE AIRCRAFT THEN TRANSMITS ITS HEIGHT OF
50 FEET WHEREUPON ANOTHER AERIAL SITUATED AT THE END OF THE RUNWAY

NALLY GUIDES THE AIRCRAFT DOWN—
IS IS OF COURSE OPERATED VIA THE AUTOMATIC PILOT

Acknowledgement to Bristol-Siddeley Journal.

A BEA Argosy 222 taking off.

the support given by post offices, especially in Australia, Britain and the United States, enabled mail to be carried at a very reasonable price. The value of the support given can be shown by the popularity of the facility; in 1933 letters from Britain to India cost 6d. for half an ounce; to send the same amount from France to South America cost 4s. 7d. This difference was not due wholly to subsidy, for both lines received one, but because the British service was well publicised, the traffic was fairly heavy and costs could be reduced.

Although mail proved to be the start of regular and intensive cargo services, it was the Second World War that proved the value of carrying freight by air. In 1948–49 the city of West Berlin was blockaded, and food, coal and the other essentials of life were all flown into the

city. Such a success has the carriage of goods by air proved, that there are now airlines, such as the American company, Seaboard World Airlines, which carry no passengers, but only freight, on its scheduled services.

The majority of freight today is still carried in the holds of ordinary passenger aircraft, although there are now many all-cargo aircraft. In most of these the freight is carried on pallets. These are flat beds, often metal, on to which the cargo is loaded and, when it has reached a certain weight or size, a net is placed over the goods to keep them on the pallet in flight. Most pallets are of one size, laid down by international agreement, which is wide enough to go into the aircraft—a large jet all-cargo freighter carries 10 or 12 pallets. If the width of the fuselage or the door is too narrow to accommodate standard pallets, smaller ones are used; one aircraft type that uses smaller pallets is the early Argosy, although later versions take standard pallets.

Once the pallet has been loaded it is carried, usually by fork-lift truck, to the aircraft and placed in the aircraft hold. It is then pushed—rollers being mounted on the aircraft for this purpose—up to the pallet previously loaded and secured to the floor. This stops the pallet moving about in the aircraft in the same way as the net stops the cargo moving on the pallet.

The Hawker Siddeley Argosy has two big advantages over other freighters. One, the fact that having full-width nose and tail doors enables loading and unloading to be carried out at the same time, has already been mentioned. The other is that the floor of the aircraft is roughly the same height as the floor of a lorry. This means that the pallet can be put on a lorry fitted with rollers, and loaded on to the aircraft from that; a small bridge being used between it and the aircraft. This saves time in loading, as the lorry can cover the distance from the cargo terminal to the aircraft much more quickly than a fork-lift truck.

One specialised form of freight carried by air is cars and the first large-scale use of air transport for ferrying cars began across the English Channel soon after the Second World War. Two companies specialised in this type operation, but these have now merged to form British United Air Ferries, which serves fourteen points in Europe and the Channel Islands from four in Britain. The Aviation Traders Carvair, a modification of the Douglas DC–4 where the cockpit is raised above the cargo area to give loading through a nose door, is used on many of these services. The Carvair is also in service linking Spain with the Balearic Islands and is used by Aer Lingus, the Irish state airline, for both car and general freight carrying duties. It can carry up to five cars and 24 passengers.

Aer Lingus Carvairs have been specially modified to carry racehorses and, indeed, the carriage of animals by air is now a common occurrence. In Europe it is not uncommon for racehorses to fly from country to country to compete in major races. Another operator who specialises in this type of work is the British independent airline, BKS Air Transport.

Nor is it only domestic animals that fly. Elephants and tigers, porpoises and poisonous snakes; all are travelling by air. The airlines have special recommendations for the diet and comfort of the animals, and special crates are needed for certain types of animal. BOAC believes that it has carried nearly every type of creature except a giraffe; it is obvious why that is the exception. There is one point of interest about the carriage of animals that is not often known. At London Airport is an R.S.P.C.A. air hostel, which is a receiving point for all kinds of animals. Since it was opened in 1952 about five million animals have passed through it.

Chi-Chi the famous Giant Panda being taken to Moscow.

Airports

Since the beginning of scheduled air services airports have developed and become more complex as the aircraft themselves have developed. A six-passenger biplane does not need as much runway for landing as a 170-passenger long-distance jet, and could quite easily do without runways altogether. Early airports were therefore often just a field with offices and hangars. As planes grew heavier, runways became needed and the standard three-runway layout became normal for airfields. Three runways laid out in a triangle enabled an aircraft to land more or less into the wind from whichever direction it was blowing.

As traffic grew heavier more runways were needed and the double-triangle layout, became popular. The ideal layout is a tangential one, with all the runways radiating at a slight angle from a central hub like the spokes of a bicycle wheel. This means that no runway crosses any other and that all runways begin at the central area where the terminal is situated. The disadvantage of this system is the very large area of land that it occupies, and the double-triangle is the best compromise between space and convenience. Here too the terminal area is best situated centrally as there is less distance for the aircraft to taxi before taking-off, or after landing.

The immediate area around every large airport is a control zone, every aircraft in the area being under supervision from the ground. These zones are linked by airways, each of which can be easily identified by its colour reference. In each airway aircraft are allotted set heights

The Super Guppy is perhaps the ugliest aircraft that has ever flown—but it is one of the most interesting. Adapted from the famous Boeing Stratocruiser it is being used to carry sections of space rockets from the manufacturing plants in California to the launching base at Cape Kennedy in Florida. The nose of this giant transport plane is hinged to allow the rocket section to be slid into the fuselage (top picture). The picture at the bottom shows the unmistakeable profile. The Super Guppy is powered by four Pratt and Witney T-34 turbo-prop motors, each producing 7,500 shaft horse power. The maximum cruising speed is 285 m.p.h., and the service ceiling of the plane is 25,000 feet.

THE SUPER GUPPY

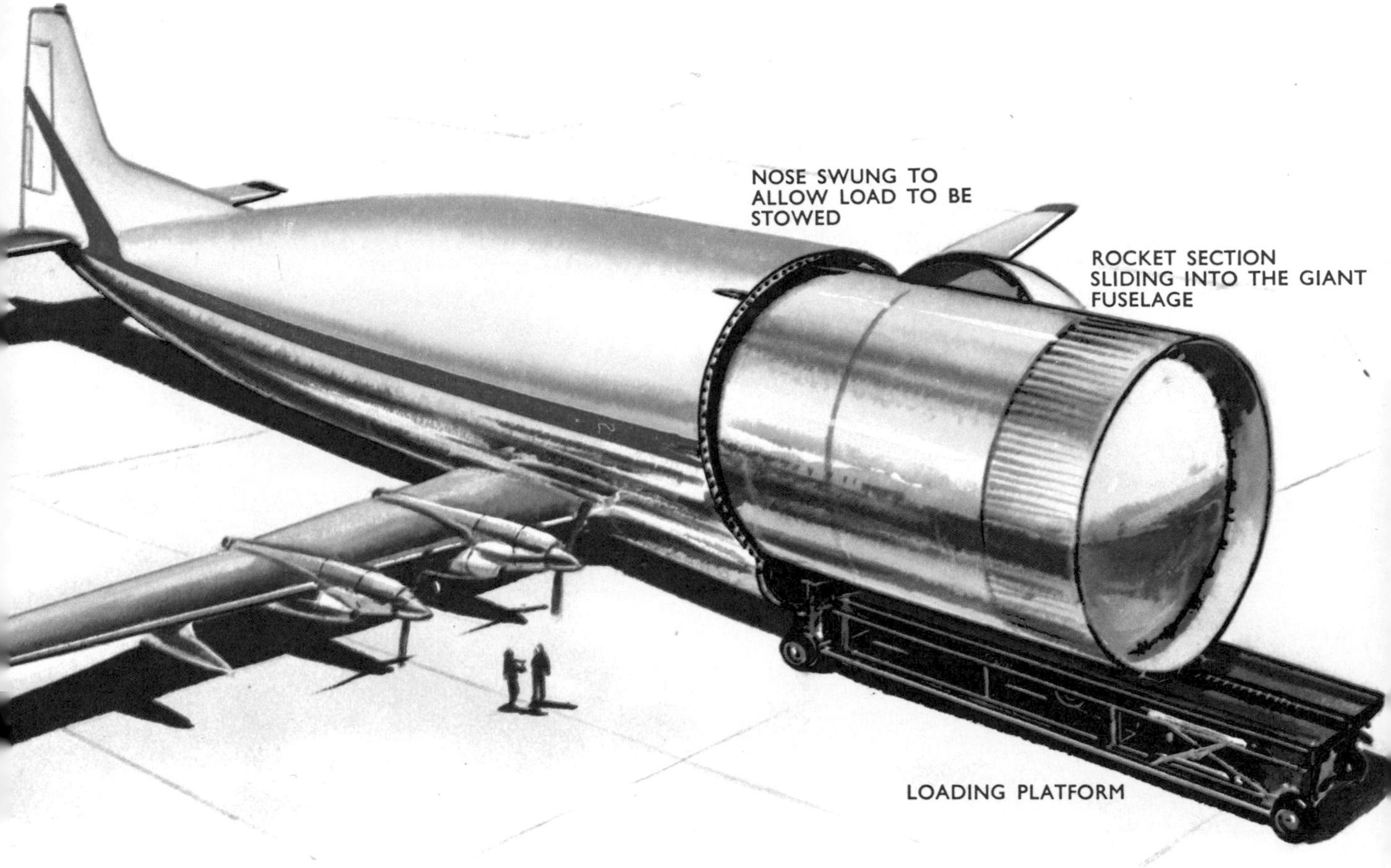

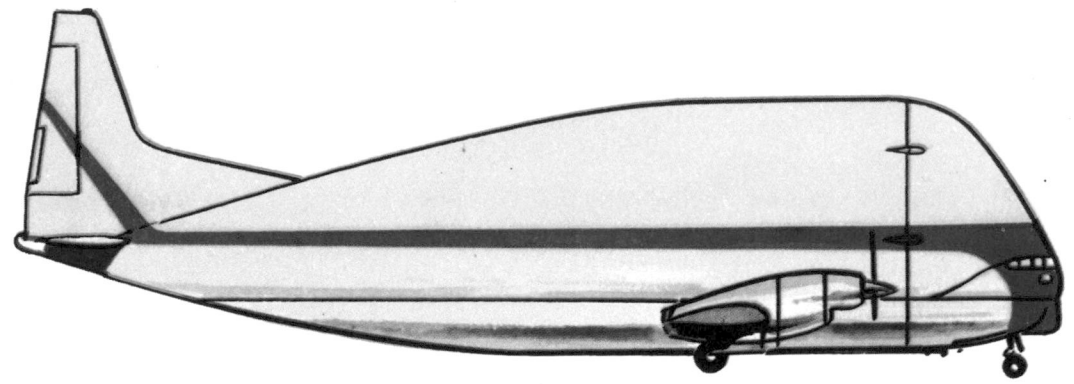

NOSE SWUNG TO
ALLOW LOAD TO BE
STOWED

ROCKET SECTION
SLIDING INTO THE GIANT
FUSELAGE

LOADING PLATFORM

SIDE ELEVATION SHOWING THE
NOSE IN CLOSED POSITION

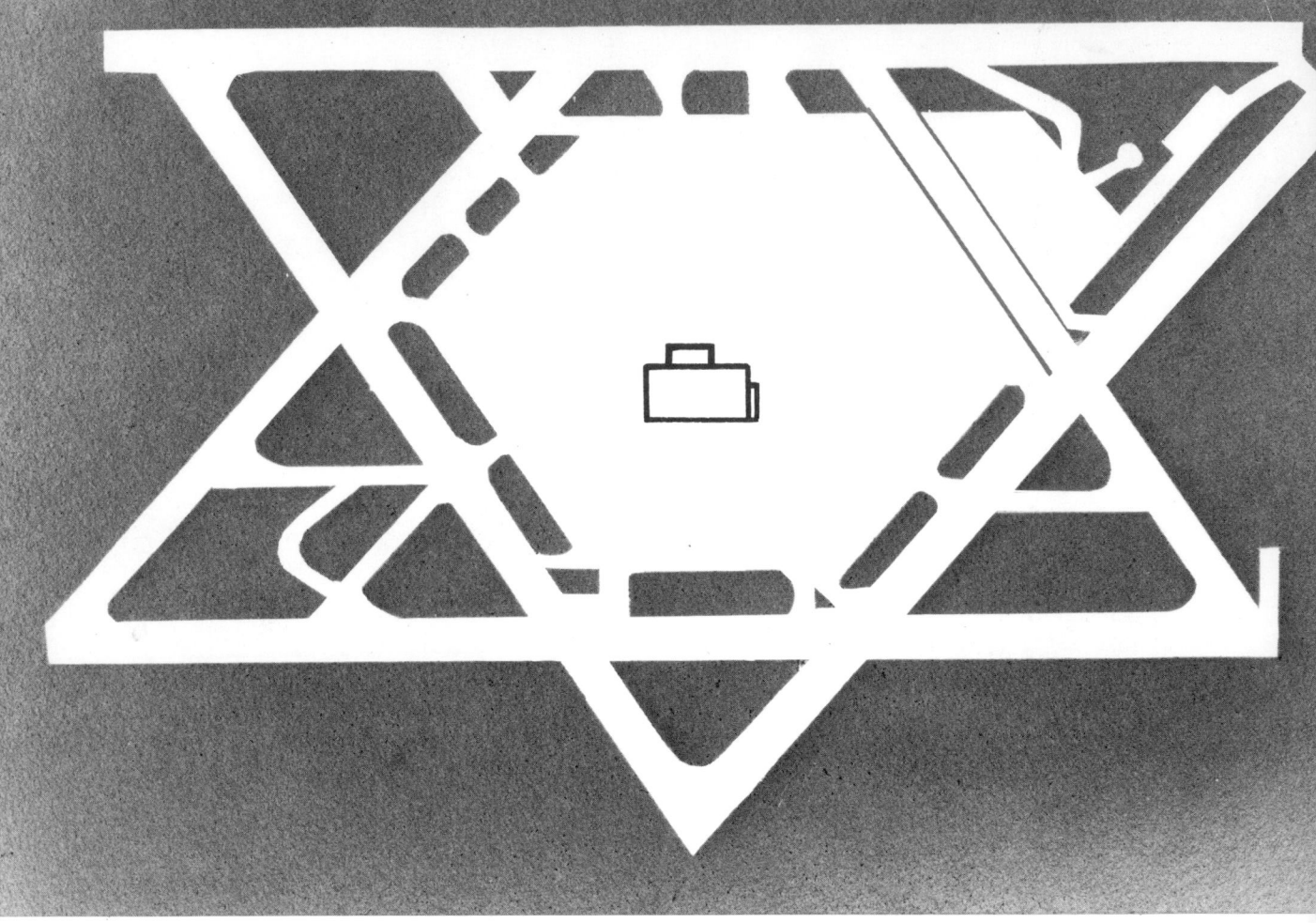

Above: The runway pattern at London (Heathrow) Airport.
Above right: The Pan American terminal at Kennedy Airport, New York.
Below right: The BEA West London Air Terminal.

136

The flight operations control centre for BEA at London Airport.

Right: The passenger pier at London Airport. In the foreground are two Trident airliners.

which they must maintain, and they have to report their position regularly to the controllers on the ground so that they can check that the aircraft is keeping the right course and altitude.

When an aircraft reaches its destination there may not be a runway free for it to land. If that is the case the aircraft has to circle round a certain point, usually a radio beacon, until it is able to land. If there are more than one aircraft waiting, they will circle the beacon at increasing heights, with the aircraft at the lowest altitude landing first and the others

descending a step, so that, for example, the next aircraft to land may be at 3,000 ft., the next one at 4,000 ft., and so on; this is called stacking.

Once the airliner has landed the passengers disembark and at many airports the traditional ways of transferring from the plane to the terminal, such as walking or by bus, have been replaced. At Washington there are mobile lounges, although these are used mainly for departing passengers. After they have completed the necessary formalities such as having their baggage weighed and their tickets

checked, passengers board this mobile lounge at first-floor level, where they can sit until the plane is ready to depart, when the mobile lounge takes them right to the plane to board it direct from a gangway. Passengers do not go into the open at all in boarding the plane.

At Amsterdam, too, passengers can board their planes without going into the open. Expanding covered bridges, known as airbridges, link the airport terminal direct to the cabin door of the aircraft.

The terminals themselves have changed recently as well. No longer is it just a

The interior of the West London Air Terminal.

place for depositing one's bags before boarding the aircraft and collecting them afterwards. Modern terminals are designed so that passengers leaving the airport do not mingle with those arriving, for this causes confusion and slows everything down. At least one airport now handles all arrivals on one floor and departures on another.

New features of air terminals are many. At Los Angeles the major airlines have separate terminals, reached only by an underground subway, which aircraft can park all around. At the Pan American terminal at the Kennedy International Airport all aircraft nose into the building, while the use of piers with aircraft parking on both sides is becoming fairly common.

If the terminals themselves are changing so are the facilities they offer. Passengers' luggage is now carried from the concourse to be loaded aboard the aircraft by conveyor belts, and waving bases for passengers' friends are also common. Now, too, many airfields have hotels near by so that passengers do not have to go into the city served by the airport to get a night's sleep or hold a business conference.

Airliners are expensive to buy—a modern transatlantic jet costs roundly £2½ million—and while on the ground they are not earning money. When an aircraft lands, therfore, every effort is made to turn it round and have it ready to leave again as quickly as possible. Apart from the passenger buses and baggage lorries, many other services are carried out in the short period between the passengers leaving the aircraft and another load embarking. These include lorries bringing the food and the fresh water, the tankers that refuel the aircraft and the vehicles that carry the cabin cleaning equipment. Although all these take time, the real factor that decides how quickly the airliner can be turned is the loading and unloading of the passengers and the time taken to refuel, as this is not

Pilots at the controls of a Comet 4B approaching Gatwick Airport.

usually permitted while passengers are entering or leaving the aircraft because of the risk of fire.

Navigating an Aeroplane

We have already mentioned the layout of runway and airport design and also the system of airways that links major airports. This is not like driving a car along a road, however, and the pilot has to rely both on his instruments and on help from the ground.

The instruments carried in an airliner are very detailed. As well as the instruments in a small aircraft, such as an airspeed indicator, an altimeter and a compass, much more detailed instruments are carried, giving details of the engine speed, the attitude of the aircraft— showing the pilot whether the aircraft is climbing, descending or banking—and many different types of navigational aids. These are only a few of the many instruments that can be seen in the photograph below.

Modern airliners carry many different types of navigational aids. One of the latest aids consists of a map, on which are marked major features of the landscape, such as airports, the coast and large towns. On this map a pen traces the aircraft's course, so that the crew can see exactly where they are at any time.

Another aid uses radio beacons, which were mentioned earlier as points over which aircraft circled while waiting to land. Each beacon gives out a different signal, so that each can be easily recognised. This particular aid consists of changeable keys, each one of which corresponds with one beacon. The pilot can switch on to one key. This automatically identifies the beacon and gives the direction and distance of the aircraft from it. By alternating between two keys, and thus between two beacons, the pilot can find out exactly where he is on a cross reference. This is a simpler method than asking for the bearing of an aircraft from two or more radio stations, with the added advantage that by this navigational aid the distance as well as the bearing is given. Both these aids are in addition to the pilot's own observations and to radar, with which every airliner is equipped both for navigation and to give the crew warning of approaching bad weather.

Radar is one of the most important advances in aircraft safety that has been made. Short-wave radio waves are sent

A flight simulator cockpit used for training pilots. Any flight condition can be realistically reproduced in this simulator, the plane can even be "crashed".

Above: A BEA Trident airliner taking off.

Below: A Viscount airliner in flight.

out from the aerial and if these hit anything they bounce back and are picked up
by the receiver. The time taken is then
halved and this gives the range and bearing of the object, which is then shown on
a screen as a speck of light. The operator
can alter the scan of the set, so that the
radar will show either everything for 50
miles or for five miles only, if a short
range is needed for an exact spot, such as
making an exact landfall after a long
ocean crossing. Some things, such as an
indented coastline or an intercontinental
airliner, will show up much better than a
two-seat training aircraft.

There are also many aids that help an
aircraft to land safely. One of the earlier
methods is Ground Control Approach,
better known as GCA. In this system,
used mainly in very poor visibility, a
lorry fitted with a radar transmitter and
receiver stands beside the runway in use.
This lorry transmits a radar beam that
picks up the aircraft and the resulting
speck of light shows up on two screens,
one of which shows the altitude of the
aircraft and the other its distance from
the transmitter. The aircraft can then be
told its position relative to the runway
and can be instructed to alter its course
or height to bring it into the best position
for landing. If the pilot wanders off-
course he is given instructions until the
aircraft appears on the radar to be flying
directly towards the runway at the correct gliding angle.

A development of GCA is automatic

Forward fuselage assembly for Lightning fighters at
BAC's Preston Works.

144

landing. This system has been under trial for some years, and a BEA Trident made the first "autoflare" landing with commercial passengers in the summer of 1965. This is a three-stage programme, autoflare being the first. With autoflare the throttles and the altitude are kept correct automatically until just before the touch-down when the pilot takes over; the change from the approach attitude to the landing attitude is also automatic. The next stage is known as "autoland", which is the same as autoflare except that the aircraft is also straightened out to align the aircraft with the runway. In the final stage, which is expected by 1970, the aircraft will be landed automatically, the brakes will be applied and the aircraft kept straight on the runway.

Although all these aids make flying much safer than it used to be, there still has to be one control for an airfield, and this is provided by the control tower. From this all the movement of aircraft in the air near the airport or on the ground, both landing or taking-off and taxying, as well as all service vehicles, is controlled. In a busy airport it would be chaotic and dangerous if there was not one central control directing all movements.

Executive Aircraft

Although air transport is usually considered to mean airliners or helicopters, there is one other type of aircraft that must be considered—the executive or business aircraft. Many aircraft constructors, especially in the United States, now build small aircraft designed for use by business men to enable them to make short journeys by air that would not be possible by airliner. These aircraft vary in size from single-engined aircraft seating 3 or 4 passengers, to 6 or 10-seat twin jet-engined aircraft such as the German-built Hansa or the Hawker Siddeley 125.

There are two big advantages for a company to have its own aircraft. Firstly, an important business man can fly between towns that are not linked by a scheduled service and, secondly, even if such a service is available he is able to travel as he wishes and not when the airline operates the flight.

Canadair CL-84 tilt-wing aircraft. Built in Canada this aircraft is designed to take off and land vertically, and yet have all the advantages of a conventional aircraft. For vertical flight and landings the wings are tilted so that the propellers act like the rotors of a helicopter. The inset shows how the wings are swung back into a normal position for forward flight. The Canadair CL-84 is powered by two Lycoming T35 turbo-shaft motors each developing 1,400 shaft-horse-power. The glass-fibre propeller blades are 14 feet in diameter. A 7-foot diameter coaxial tail rotor is fitted at the rear to keep the aircraft stable during vertical flight.

146

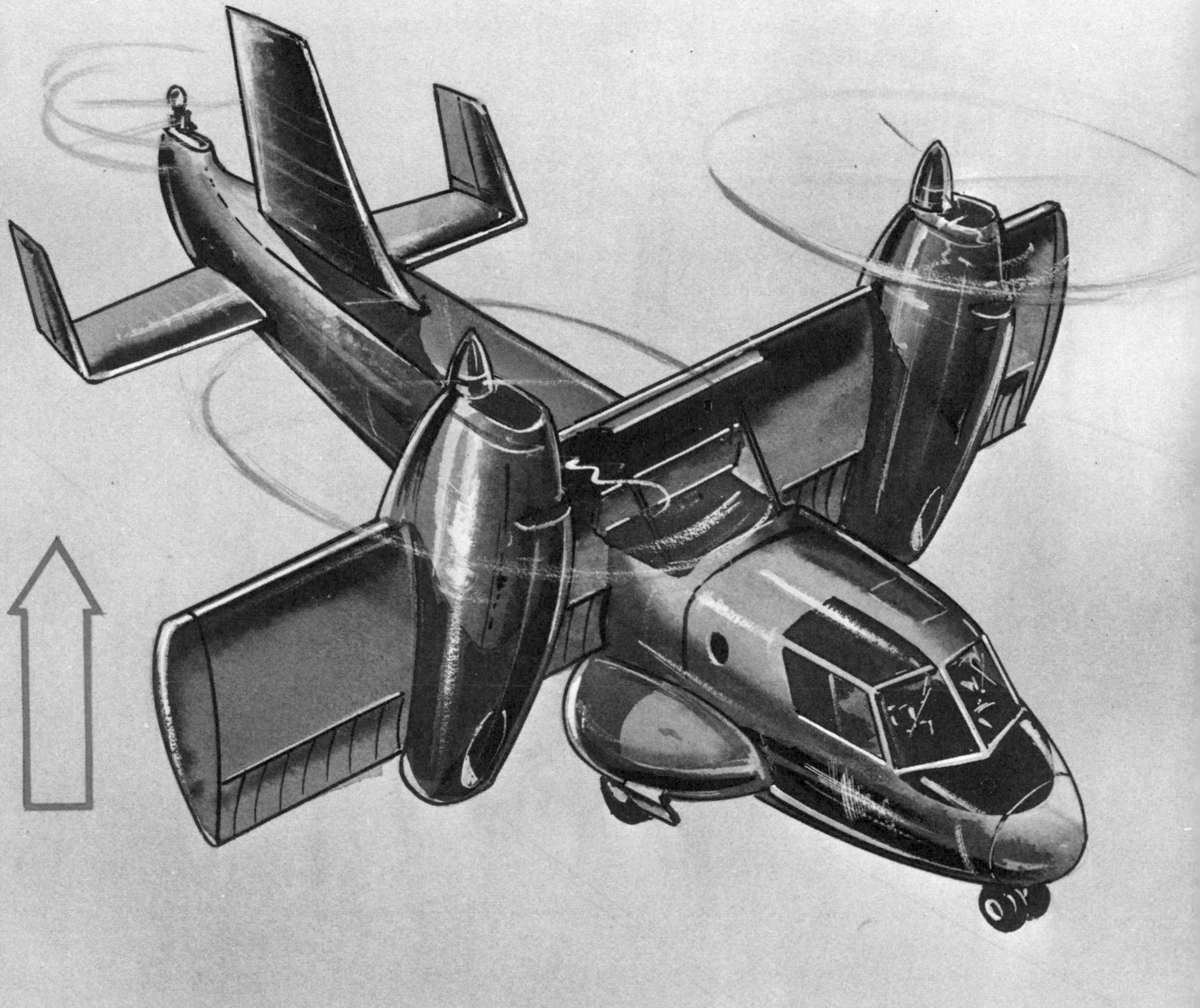

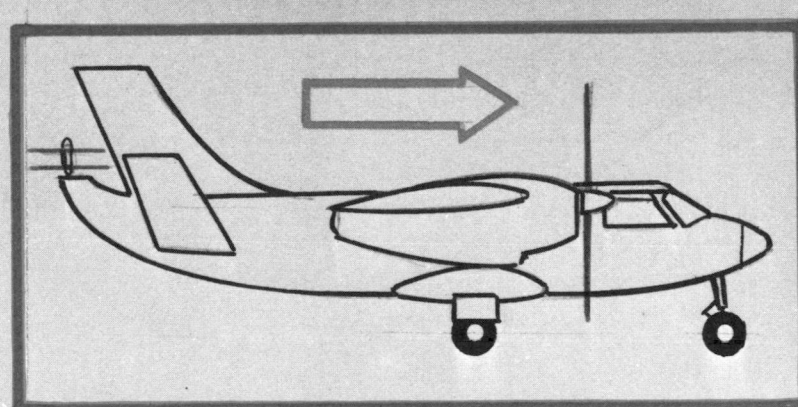

THE WINGS OF THIS AIRCRAFT
SWIVEL THROUGH 90° ENABLING
THE AIRSCREW TO ACT LIKE ROTORS
ON A HELICOPTER WHEN THEY
ARE IN THE POSITION SHOWN
IN THE DRAWING ABOVE.
THE INSET (LEFT) SHOWS HOW
THE WINGS RESUME THE NORMAL
POSITION OF A CONVENTIONAL
AIRCRAFT TO ATTAIN FORWARD
FLIGHT.

Future of Air Transport

We have now covered briefly air transport today, but what of tomorrow? The Wright brothers made their successful flight a mere sixty years ago. To look forward sixty years would be fantasy; forty years would be guesswork; twenty years would be unwise—so fast is progress.

In ten years' time supersonic transports will be operating all the major long-haul air routes, with regular services from the airport to the city centre by 50-seat helicopters running like a bus service. Vertical take-off and landing jet aircraft will be operating on shorter routes between the centres of cities themselves and turboprop aircraft will be used only for very short flights. Helicopters will be used even more than now for all purposes, and the larger firms will operate their own light aircraft, and possibly even small helicopters. Air transport will expand greatly in the next ten or twenty years in the same way as the railways did in the middle of the last century.

Rockets and Space Flight

The origin of the rocket is lost in time and its inventor is unknown. It is known that a powderlike mixture was used to drive arrows forward to speed up their flight. The freely rising rocket as a weapon of war was apparently first invented by the Chinese in the thirteenth century. These early rockets were powered by gunpowder and it was not long before they found their way into Europe. They were used in warfare for many centuries.

The modern rocket was developed by the American Robert H. Goddard who began his experiments soon after the 1914–18 war. Goddard dropped the idea of using powder rockets and became interested in the use of liquid fuels. Some of his ideas were later used by the Germans in experimental rockets before the Second World War.

Although rocket experiments, including some with freight-carrying rockets, continued between the world wars, the first really successful rocket was the German V2. Carrying a high-explosive charge, this weapon was launched against London and other cities. The V2 reached a height of 60 miles and had a speed of 3,400 m.p.h. It was 46 ft. long and weighed 12 tons, of which the explosive warhead weighed 1 ton and the fuel 8 tons.

After the end of the war the United States and Russia became the two countries chiefly concerned with their development. By the early 1950s the design of rockets using liquid-fuel had been greatly developed and the early intercontinental ballistic missiles or ICBMs were being designed. Their progress was rapid, and by the late 1950s these rockets were being launched regularly on trial flights.

The conquest of space really began in October, 1957, when the Russians launched the first man-made satellite, Sputnik 1, and followed it a month later with Sputnik 2, which weighed half-a-ton and carried a dog as a passenger. In the following March the Americans launched their first satellite, Vanguard 1.

In August, 1960, the Russians launched a satellite, called Sputnik 5, which contained two dogs and other living creatures, into space and recovered it satisfactorily. In April of the following

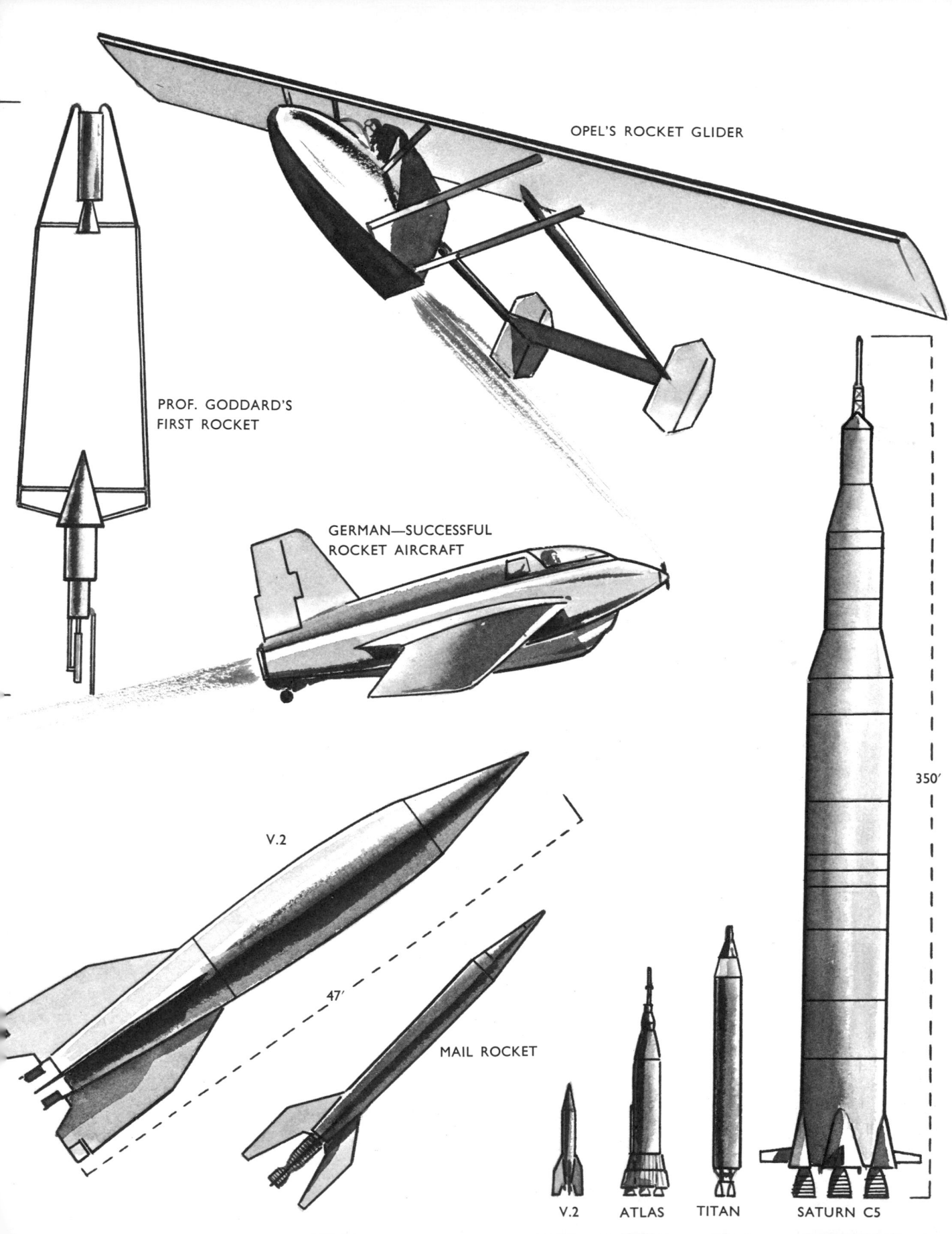

OPEL'S ROCKET GLIDER

PROF. GODDARD'S
FIRST ROCKET

GERMAN—SUCCESSFUL
ROCKET AIRCRAFT

V.2

47´

MAIL ROCKET

350´

V.2   ATLAS   TITAN   SATURN C5

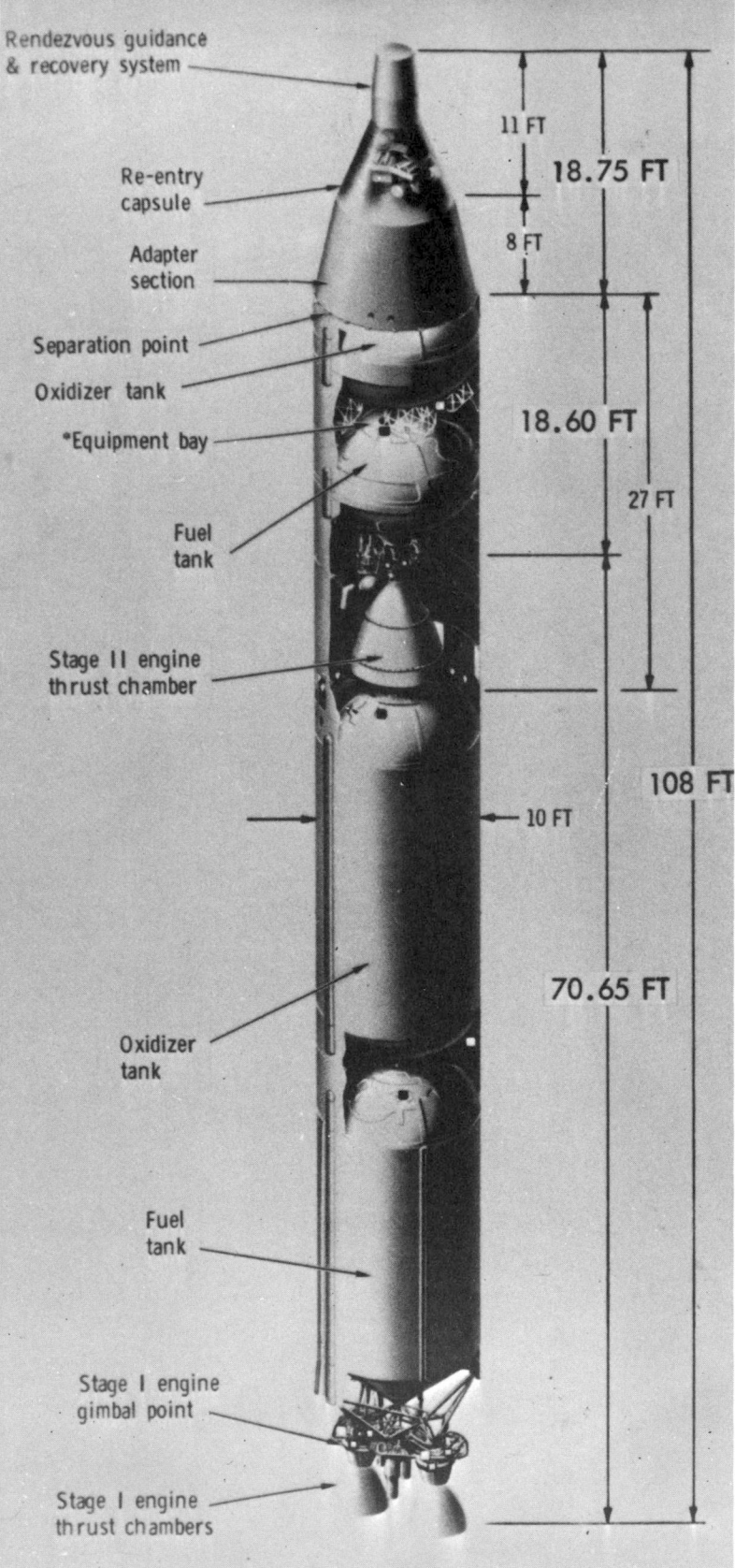

Rendezvous guidance & recovery system

Re-entry capsule

Adapter section

Separation point

Oxidizer tank

*Equipment bay

Fuel tank

Stage II engine thrust chamber

Oxidizer tank

Fuel tank

Stage I engine gimbal point

Stage I engine thrust chambers

11 FT

18.75 FT

8 FT

18.60 FT

27 FT

108 FT

10 FT

70.65 FT

year, Major Yuri Gagarin made one orbit of the earth in Vostok 1 and landed safely. Since then the Russians have achieved many successes in manned space flight including having two manned spacecraft in orbit at the same time and putting the first woman into space. In October, 1964, they launched Voskhod 1, the first three-man spacecraft, and in March, 1965, A. Leonov became the first man actually to go into space, when he spent 10 minutes outside his craft while it was in orbit.

While the United States has also been developing manned satellites, they have been giving more attention than the Russians to communications satellites, to which we will return later. The first United States manned space flights did not place the astronaut into orbit; that is to say that although he was in space he did not circle the earth. These early

Titan II Rocket and Gemini capsule for the first two-man Gemini flight in space.
*The equipment bay contains: batteries; malfunction detection system; range safety command control system; programmer; radio guidance system; auto pilot; instrumentation and telemetry system.

A Gemini Capsule showing the astronaut "walking in space".

United States suborbital flights were of about 3,000 miles only down a "rocket range" into the South Atlantic.

In February, 1962, John Glenn made the first United States orbital flight in a Mercury capsule and other United States astronauts have also orbited the earth, Gordon Cooper achieving 22 orbits. In March, 1965, the first American two-man space flight took place, when Virgil Grissom and John Young made three orbits in a Gemini capsule. In December, 1965, Frank Borman and James Lovell achieved a total of 206 orbits in a flight lasting nearly 14 days. This was the longest space flight achieved up to that time and James Lovell has spent more time in space than any other man. On the last Gemini flight Edwin Aldrin spent $5\frac{1}{2}$ hours in space outside the capsule in three separate excursions. In this time he carried out experiments on working in space and took photographs.

Both the United States and Russia have also achieved many notable results from unmanned spacecraft. The first successes were by the Russians, who, in 1959, hit the moon with Lunik 2 and later the same year successfully sent television pictures of the hidden face of the moon back from Lunik 3; these were taken from a height of about 40,000 miles. With their Ranger probes the Americans have been transmitting television pictures back to earth as the satellite falls towards the surface of the moon. The closest picture yet obtained was taken from Ranger 9 at an altitude of 2,400 ft., only 0·4 seconds before impact. Craters as small as 5 ft. in diameter were clearly visible.

The United States has also sent probes to Mars and Venus to learn more about those two planets than we know at present. Mariner 2, which passed close by Venus in December, 1962, sent back information which suggested that Venus had a temperature of 800 degrees Fahrenheit and an atmosphere with no oxygen or water. In July, 1964, Mariner IV passed close to Mars and sent back many pictures of the planet's surface. In addition, these and other space probes also sent back such details as the density of meteorites and the strength of cosmic rays.

It is in telecommunications that the United States seems to have achieved a lead over the Russians. The first satellite for intercontinental television transmissions was Telstar, and this was followed by Relay, another low-altitude orbiting satellite. Early Bird, which is in use at present, is the first commercial communications satellite. Situated at a stationary

A movable rocket launching platform, 'Tread Monster'. Its immense size is indicated by comparison with the six-wheel truck alongside. Its eight tractor treads are powered by two Diesel engines.

Left: Rear view of Gemini 7 as seen by Gemini 6 astronauts.

Right: The Gemini 12 lift-off from Cape Kennedy on Nov. 11, 1966. James Lovell and Edwin Aldrin completed a 59-orbit mission which included a 2 hour walk in space.

Astronaut Edward White during his 20-minute walk in space during the third orbit of Gemini 4. He used a hand-held jet gun to assist his movements. Edward White was one of three astronauts killed in the tragic accident at Cape Kennedy when an Apollo capsule caught fire.

position 22,300 miles above the Atlantic at the Equator south-west of the Ivory Coast, it can provide both two-way television and telephone channels between Europe and North America. Other American satellites are used for weather forecasting, to aid navigation of ships at sea and to obtain information on the radiation belts that circle the earth.

Having looked at the satellites themselves we can now turn to the rockets that launch them. It is possible, however, only to discuss the United States rockets—the Russians have said very little about their launch vehicles—and those of the European Launcher Development Organisation, usually referred to as ELDO. This is a combined organisation in which seven European countries are taking part and in which each of the three stages of the satellite-launching rocket is being constructed in a different country.

In a three-stage rocket the first section of the configuration launches the rocket, and when this has climbed as far as it can, the motor of the second stage takes over, the first stage being jettisoned. The same is true of the second and third stages, the latter leaving the satellite in orbit.

The most advanced United States rocket is the two-stage Saturn C–IB, which can put 32,000 lb. into a low orbit around the earth. It will be followed by the Saturn C–5, which will be able to put 120 tons into low orbit or 35 tons on a planetary mission. The largest American missile planned is the Nova, which will be able to put about 300 tons into an earth orbit. Nova will be used for taking passengers and cargo to the moon and into orbit around the earth for establishing and supplying space stations.

In 1968 the United States plans to have a two-man space laboratory in orbit around the earth in which the crew

The Agena target vehicle pictured during the flight of Gemini 12.

will be able to live for up to a month. The crew of the 8-ton laboratory will change on a shift basis using two-man Gemini spacecraft.

Both Russia and the United States hope to have men on the moon in the next three years. The Apollo project is planned to place three United States astronauts in orbit around the moon, from which two will detach from the orbiting satellite in a small capsule to explore the moon's surface; it is hoped that this will take place in 1970. Both countries have been successful in putting unmanned craft on the moon.

Later expeditions will explore the moon more thoroughly and before the end of the century man will probably have reached the nearer planets. What he will find no one knows, but one thing is certain. Whatever the difficulties, the transport industry, which has solved so many problems in the past, will be able to help. As man has developed so has his transport, for without transport there can be no development.

INDEX

LAND TRANSPORT

(The Darker Page Numbers Indicate Illustrations)

157